*Words have power. So do lies.
The solution to most common problems
rests upon one question:
Is it true?*

A Culture
of LIES

SYLVIE NOMENY

DEDICATION

To my two sweet angels, my AmFar stars, whom I love dearly.

To all the people who have been presumed guilty before being found innocent.

I am grateful for the stones thrown that made this cornerstone and the lemons that made this lemonade possible.

© 2024 Sylvie Nomeny
AmFar Publishing

No part of this publication may be reproduced, distributed, or transmitted in any form or by any means, including photocopying, recording, or other electronic or mechanical methods, or by any information storage and retrieval system without the prior written permission of the publisher, except in the case of very brief quotations embodied in critical reviews and certain other noncommercial uses permitted by copyright law.

For more information, email Sylvie at sylvieserge.nt@hotmail.com

ISBN: 979-8-9918794-0-8 (paperback)
ISBN: 979-8-9918794-1-5 (eBook)

Library of Congress Control Number: 2024923290

Cover Design by Kelly Nielsen, Studio 92
Interior and e-book formatting by Amit Dey

TABLE OF CONTENTS

Preface vii

1. History of Lies and Skepticism 1
2. What is the Truth? 19
3. The Boundless Motivation of Lies 33
4. Lying Shall be Illegal 65
5. An Affliction to Society 73
6. The Power of Words and Lies 93
7. The Impacts of Lies 113
8. How Lying Affects Character 129
9. The Physical and Emotional Effects of Lies. . . 149
10. The Importance of Due Diligence 159

About the Author 173

Connect with the Author 175

PREFACE

*Think about this assessment:
1% of the population controls the world,
4% of the population may be the instruments of the
1%, 90% of the population are sleeping zombies.
While 5% of the population try to wake up the sleeping
zombies, Then, the 1% makes sure that the 4% stop
the 5% from waking up the 90% of the population.
This can only be achieved by the 4 % perpetrating fear
with lies toward the 90%, to divide and conquer, then
to gain and maintain power.*

We hear a lot about lying, and even more so in modern day communications. Everyone says everything, the truth and the lies. Politicians say whatever they need to say to get elected. The marketing industry is dominated by lies; advertisers say whatever they can to make a profit. Criminals insist they did not commit the crimes they were caught doing. Actors and community leaders lie to keep their positive public image. Even the people close to us, relatives and friends, say whatever they can to save face while tarnishing their peers. Just like an animal might deceive other members of its group about where it found food for its survival and then must remember where it found the food while deceiving others, humans similarly tell a lie to explain another lie they told.

In many situations, the term "lying" might not actually be total deception. "Lying" is a term for telling something completely false to obtain a desired outcome. It does not include disagreement about interpretations or lack of context. Telling a lie also does not fully cover situations where shared material supports a point, but material not supporting the point is left out. Lies are totally, or almost totally, false and typically have a specific purpose of deceiving another individual, as opposed to getting them to change their point of view or at least consider another's point of view. "Lying" is a serious term that tends to bring discussions to a halt by essentially taking away all validity of the arguments. Certainly, lying has become more pervasive in modern society than ever, with the advent of followers following a crowd without question. Education may have failed critical thinking. Whether that is the case or not is up for debate. There may be more reasons to hear lies and question what we hear, yet there are many opportunities to catch people in untruths as useful mischief.

There is a real science behind the reasons people tell lies and the difference in the types of lies they tell, either to save face or to serve their desires and/or wishes for good or bad deeds. No one likes to be lied to or about, and most people do not consider themselves liars since lying has become prevalent in modern culture, to the point of killing the taboo aspect of it. Those who do so easily get away with their mischief and often exploit the slackness of any due diligence by the majority, the sleeping zombies, the followers, and the 90% of the population that will be the focus of this narration, with individual understanding of a lie. Therefore, others become guilty only by accusation or guilty by association because we fail to ask one question: Is it true? And if we do, finding an answer that avoids a crisis will be possible.

Through years of experience as a law person and a layperson, I have come to understand that society and the world are made of lies from all corners. I believe that people are presumed innocent until proven guilty, but society has assumed the opposite, where one is guilty until proven innocent. And the return to that innocent status can be difficult even if later proven by all things true.

The *Ten Commandments* teaches honesty and integrity among other values and morals. Almost everyone was taught not to make false statements, and the teaching clearly makes total sense and even more so today, not because lies do not exist or have some impact in our life, but because we shall be more careful with what we say and what we are told. Lies appear to be at the center of every single problem in society, and whether we realize it or not, we are all affected by them. But a solution to a better and peaceful society starts with us; it begins with one simple question: Is it true?

As one of the many about whom false stories have been made up and uttered around, I created this book, not to focus on myself and my personal trauma or pain surrounding lies, though I can relate to most of the examples cited along. I created this book to explore what motivates people to lie; and understanding when, why, and how they lie is crucial. Discussion about a lie often seems like a forbidden subject, a taboo, as if there is no such thing as a lie; nevertheless, lying always brings so much to question. Of course, the word "lie" sounds like shame itself, yet many people do lie. They tell a lie to make their way or break others' way.

I created this book to help understand our surroundings, establish a more comprehensive communication, and warn about what threatens meaningful relationships. While we are all affected by lies, a solution begins with one simple question: Is it true? This book will take you to when and how you can be part of the solution. Hopefully, this can prevent some ruination from happening due to being falsely informed and, therefore, building a more truthful and peaceful culture.

As we begin,

> *"One thing took deep root in me, the conviction that morality is the basis of things, and that truth is the substance of all morality."*
>
> — Mahatma Gandhi

Let us get started…

1
HISTORY OF LIES AND SKEPTICISM

"A lie will go round the world while the truth is pulling its boots on."

— Spurgeon,
an English fundamentalist Baptist Preacher

The message in this book is a reminder to readers to always question what they hear, to always question the purpose behind any telltale, to verify any information received, and most importantly, not to use false or unverified information to take a position, or to reach any decision or judgment. Perhaps honesty cannot be forced on people. This is not the mission of this book, but honesty and justice are good for society and should be taught. It starts with oneself. It starts with telling the truth. It starts with refraining from reaching conclusions based on unverified information or on a lie. It starts with first asking yourself, is it true?

The teaching of Socrates can be summarized by the words 'question everything.' Socrates lived his life questioning every assumption or piece of wisdom people around him believed was the truth. According to Socrates, truth is an objective and absolute reality that exists independently of human perception or belief. It is not subjective or relative, but it is something that can be discovered through rational inquiry and critical thinking. Truth is what transpires from facts, not an opinion, and society can be beautiful and peaceful if everyone can "question everything." And questioning begins with skepticism.

People are undoubtedly driven by suspicion, curiosity, and wonder. How do you decide what to believe in your life? It is the question we ask that fuels and guides our thinking. Many problems arise from making assumptions. In other words, if you assume, you think you know when you probably do not. At its core, skepticism is the art of questioning. Skepticism is the ability to withhold judgment until all the evidence is provided, allowing a person to look at the situation or actions somewhat carefully. While many may view skepticism as pessimistic or negative, questioning everything can be a powerful tool for truth, knowledge, progress, growth, justice, and peace.

Skepticism dates back to the philosophers of ancient Greece, including Sextus Empiricus and Pyrrho, who focused on the concept that actual knowledge was hard to come by. Pyrrho advocated for the suspension of judgment over the truth of all beliefs. Also, during the scientific revolution, thinkers like Rene Descartes and Francis Bacon emphasized the importance of skepticism in pursuing knowledge. Annas and Barnes' outlines of skepticism in the Cambridge University Press clearly explain the concept. Thus, those philosophers argued that we should suspend judgments on all matters because knowledge was uncertain.

In other words, putting equal weight on opposing arguments leads us to equipollence, which means similar or equivalent in power, effect, or significance. As reality demonstrates, truth and lies are opposing ends of a conversation and they are neither similar nor equivalent. Bury cited, in Cambridge University Press, the example of Pyrrho who took the concept of equipollence to the extreme and would not decide what to eat or wear, believing that he could not be sure about his right or wrong choices.

On the other hand, Sextus Empiricus believed he could gather knowledge through experience and practical observations. He argued that we should not rely on logical deduction or abstract reasoning alone, which could lead to a wrong path or decision. Instead, we should observe the world around us and draw conclusions based on our experiences and what we see. Descartes believed that we should doubt everything, including our existence, until it could be proven without a shadow of a doubt. His extreme skepticism made him doubt the presence of the external world. In their

A Contemporary Reader, on this skepticism, DeRose and Warfield taught that the only thing Descartes believed was his existence as a 'thinking being,' expressed in the phrase, "I think, therefore I am."

While these famous thinkers may sound extreme or radical in their thinking, their skepticism can serve as a practical tool that stretches our understanding of truth. Dearly missed are the days when society followed the path of thoughts set by these famous thinkers. Whether they were extreme or radical did not matter. What mattered was the truth. Their exceptional examples were golden, and the contemporaneous world seems to have lost them.

Spurgeon's statement was not only history. It was valid centuries ago as it is still valid today, because skepticism may mean waiting for the truth. One Tanzanian proverb reminds us that "the path of a liar is very short," meaning that a lie has a short life, but truth lives on forever. And that embraces the biblical perspective, while the proverb underlines the importance of truthfulness. The proverb can be translated into our daily lives. Whether the path of a liar is a defense mechanism or a sense of protection, it is a lie, and the vulnerability that comes with just believing in it, makes it seem true.

While asking questions and keeping an open mind have positive effects in seeking the truth, there is a dark side to constantly feeling uncertain about what you hear and being extremely skeptical. Uncertainty promotes being stuck in a situation by never deciding to move on and figuring out what is true and what is not. Because we constantly evaluate the situation and question what we should or should not do, procrastination keeps us in skepticism mode. This becomes problematic when a quick decision may be required, or in the situation of an emergency. However, lack of trust may cause excessive doubt as it hinders collaboration or even damages a relationship in the process.

Skepticism being another aspect of doubt, it is essential to understand the difference between healthy skepticism and cynicism. Cynicism is often tainted by general negativity and distrust of others, while skepticism revolves around questioning and evaluating the evidence. When it comes to seeking the truth, skepticism and cynicism play a role. Striking a balance between the two is critical to maintaining a willingness to consider all perspectives. This is very helpful when time is of the essence, such as when making a time-sensitive decision with the information at hand, and what has been told. Thus, time-sensitive decision-making does not negate getting to the truth.

Nonetheless, focus can be put on the potential outcomes of each decision to be made by weighing the pros and cons, which helps to consider the risks and the benefits of a doubt in a given situation. It helps to make an informed decision and to take a position without being bogged down by undue or extreme doubt. Skepticism helps in a powerful way in strengthening relationships essentially in everyday lives. Yet it requires wisdom to be skeptical, with critical thinking as moderator, questioning what we hear, keeping an open mind, and being aware of all the downsides. Skepticism helps to mature our understanding of contemporaneous pressures, but a balanced approach of being skeptical is beneficial to all circumstances.

The many benefits of being skeptical and questioning any information are countless.

Think about the following:

The evolution of human intelligence is filled with an ability to keep an open mind, to learn new ideas, and observe new situations amongst other things. Such an ability can also foster tolerance without discounting understanding for the new people who come into our lives with different points of view. Most importantly, such an ability helps to gather all the facts before forming an opinion or making a judgment. Very often, in a conversation that challenges political beliefs for example, rather than dismissing another's viewpoint, it is open-minded to weigh it against our existing beliefs and others' carefully. An open mind allows a better understanding of different thoughts and perspectives and promotes acceptance and tolerance. Keeping an open mind and welcoming new ideas does not discount weighing on the accuracy of the idea or situation and its effectiveness. And to keep an open mind, the first question remains: is it true?

All things considered, being skeptical can be a valuable tool for navigating this complex world by encouraging critical thinking and fostering tolerance while promoting an open mind. In today's world of the internet and social media, we are inundated with information of all sorts, and it becomes a challenge to determine what is true, what is not, and even what is 'fake news,' to quote others. Modern politics appears as a sandbox of open-minded games where false information and 'fake news' dominate to manipulate the masses. And modern relations become the victims and casualties of such games. For sure, relationships of all nature suffer from lies, the false information that internet and social media can spread, adding to what a person may use, with the goal to manipulate and destroy.

Unfortunately, and politically, we have come to a place where lies become a tool of politics that influence opinions. Though many have closed their mind to one ideology only by hearing and going along and following a crowd or believing without asking if it is true, when we separate facts from fiction, truth from lies, false from accurate information, we do ourselves a favor by asking questions and evaluating what we read and hear from anyone before taking a position. When we do, we are a step away from finding what is true, while saving what can be destroyed with a lie. And we are closer to making judgment based on the facts proven to be true, not on fiction of what we are told. How often do we get away from a relationship when we are told a lie about such a relation? How often do we get away from opportunities when we do not consider it an opportunity but instead focus on the lie that we are told? How often do we get buyer's remorse after having cast a vote based on the lies of politicians only to find out to have voted against self-interest? How often do we get buyer's remorse after spending an amount of money on a product that is not what we thought it was, because the advertisement told us so? It is often helpful to do some research to overcome some emotions provoked by manipulative information before making a judgment, a purchase, or even casting a vote. Livelihood and the future may depend on it.

Every now and then, a product is recalled for not being what it was described and advertised to be after research, verification, and due diligence have played out, and lies or perhaps mistakes were discovered. Unfortunately, when the truth always comes last, side effects have already kicked in: people have lost money, and others have made money. In short, the damage has already been done. At the end of the day, it is about the effects of lies when no one asks, is it true? How many people believe in 'ads' during election season? Unfortunately, many do, at their own peril. It is wiser to read the policies, get educated in them, look at the past experiences and present realities, instead of listening to political advertising that is often more destructive, even mentally.

The Harvard Review noted that when President Jimmy Carter asked the 400 largest corporations to limit wage and price increases to contain inflation in 1978, most Ford Motor executives thought the move would worsen inflation. Ford issued a statement welcoming the president's initiative and strategically endorsing his goal. Although the president's guidelines and the pricing plans did not match, calling for significant increase, the company supported the program. Ford's image makers decided that publicly opposing the anti-inflation effort would be politically dangerous. They hoped that the company's seeming support would help restrain its suppliers from increasing prices and its workers from demanding higher wages. Ford's statement may have been a cynical lie, intentionally or not. This makes us believe that the press did not play its role to report useful and accurate information but to promote private privilege and public illusion, not to exclude individual responsibility for due diligence.

Evaluating the information that we receive, and the evidence we can find, becomes capital to solidifying the validity of the information. It helps to develop a deeper understanding of situations and the culture as a whole. Making informed and intelligent decisions becomes essential. This critical exercise should guide our daily lives, even on a small scale, like shopping in the grocery store. For example, the products that we see labeled "All Natural" or "100% Organic," although it is normal to think those products are in fact organic or all natural because the company may be in compliance with some food and drug regulations, there can be a question whether these claims are true. But the main belief is that they are, just by reading the labels, thus it can be difficult and time consuming for due diligence, because of its scale status. Thus, evaluating information should be a daily assignment, and the evidence uncovered allows us to make informed decisions on whether or not the product can be selected.

Also, imagine hearing that this specific person is awful, and repeatedly, day in and day out, someone you have never met, but can be in charge of your life or activities directly and indirectly, someone who believes himself or herself to be the sincerest person to ever meet. The repeated line alone may ignite your critical mind about what it said, what you heard, and what you believe. Your position may depend on the accuracy of what you have heard whether you believe in what you hear with no question, or you may want to question if what you are told is accurate. Paying attention to the media, or participating in a discussion that highlights opposing views, may make you question and question again. Imagine hearing that X is a "racist" person, especially from people that dislike or have no sympathy for X. Maybe X is not actually "racist," but rather they simply want the whole world to turn against X; and make sure that none ever like X, purchase from X, or even vote for X. What if it was not true? Words that are awful, like 'racist' for example, can be used to negatively malign a person, yet many people use those to chase away or cut from their peers. This reminds me of once being portrayed as a villain to people I did not know, that I have never met, and for things I knew nothing about, yet it often works in social discourse. Of course, lies stick with telling and telling again. Thus, when I am told that someone is awful or is doing something he or she should not be doing, I ask myself, is it true? Unfortunately, most people do not. Not because it will make a person look like a villain, but because it changes something, no matter what it could be, it can be a perception of what is.

Because humans are interconnected, relationships are an important aspect of life, and actions and choices can have a ripple effect on the world we live in, including how we communicate, what we say, what we hear, and what we believe. At an individual level, being skeptical gives us a step back to better assess how to communicate with others, approaching individual relationships with attention, curiosity, kindness and compassion. With that, it becomes easy to understand people's behaviors, and therefore, avoid false assumptions that lead to a trap of lies. However, to question assumptions is part of nurturing the relationship, which can help reshape attitudes toward others, make better judgments or consider alternatives. Also, keeping an open mind means nurturing good relationships when we refrain from taking positions about others by hearing and believing only.

No matter the type of relationship at stake, whether with a spouse, colleague, a significant other, friends or relatives, honesty is the most critical aspect of those relationships. The honesty factor can differentiate between salvaging, strengthening, dismantling, or ruining the relationship. Remember the saying, "What a tangled web we weave," which has many meanings.

It may mean it takes multiple dishonest acts or lies to create a domino structure before we lose control of the consequences. It may also mean that when a lie is told about a lie, to explain how a lie is not a lie, it becomes a tangled web, a multitude of dishonest acts. But it does not mean that if you tell a lie constantly, it will necessarily turn into a monstrous web of deceit. Honesty becomes the best way to strengthen a relationship, and it starts with being truthful.

Let us say someone tells a lie that hurts, directly or indirectly, intentionally or unintentionally. The wise thing to do would be to communicate what caused the pain, because the person may not be aware of any wrongdoing. But too often, people try to protect themselves from being hurt even more and give the benefit of the doubt, then continue to live silently with the pain and nothing is done. It could be that the person who did the hurting will want to protect himself and is unwilling to admit any wrongdoing either. Whatever the situation may be, keeping a positive mindset and finding a psychological balance of strength helps alleviate the hurt. Ultimately, what was a relationship may become an acquaintanceship, because whenever a person does not acknowledge a wrongdoing, he is deemed to repeat it, and a solution may be to part ways or retreat.

Nevertheless, a person who finds nothing wrong with lying will continue to do so, and at the end of the day, the purpose behind the lies continues. It may not be intentional, but most of the time, it is. Very often, the goal of making such lies may not only be to manipulate the audience, but to upset or keep the victim upset, to degrade and destroy something, no matter what. And the ripple effect is to break any trust in relationships. It creates turmoil. It divides and keeps people apart from each other. Also, the purpose may be to destroy one's image because lies do such, and it does not matter to the lying person how far it goes or whatever it takes. Unfortunately, it becomes very difficult to want to maintain a relationship in such situations once a break in trust occurs.

Certainly, it is difficult to resolve a disagreement at the breaking point, if pent-up feelings sit with a person aggravating the situation. At some point, the perpetrator's relentlessness exposes their personality and what they want: nothing but to keep others in a state of hurt and upset, if not diminished. At that point, creating a healthy distance and seeking essential protection is a good way out. It often does not matter what type of relationship is attacked, affected, or damaged; sometimes, health, sanity, and peace trump maintaining some hurtful relationships for the sake of belonging.

Whether it is a defense mechanism or a sense of protection, a lie preys on the vulnerability that comes with just believing in it, making it seem true. Imagine someone trying to convince everyone, mostly the vulnerable, to align with his desires, simply relying on something unfounded. It may not seem important if the desires do not align with others. But it is a big deal to mislead others to follow the desires of the misleader, because his wishes are their command. Unfortunately, the gullible make this mistake and alignment all the time. Sadly, lies play a role, a bad one, but truth makes a difference. .

Besides, truth characterizes integrity and often honesty, although truth and honesty are two different things. In a peaceful state of mind, the more secure and confident people become, the more reason they have to be honest and tell the truth, and the less reason they have to lie. This is something most people have a problem with, because it hides some fear. It is often a diversion from one point of view. Nevertheless, telling something that is not true may include unnecessary tales that destroy honesty, integrity and even confidence in self. And definitely, truthfulness, honesty, integrity and confidence routinely nurture good deeds.

As good as it can be, if honesty can be included in what a good relationship means, it should go both ways. Honesty should be a give and take, and expectations from others depend on it. Being honest makes people think positively to exclude the possibility to tell a lie. Being honest may appear as being vulnerable, but the two characteristics collide with what is the truth. Vulnerability can also put people in an awkward place, especially when caring about the people we love, by being truthful. This is part of the battle of recognizing unhealthy relationships but staying in it for the sake of peace as a coping mechanism, because telling the truth can be a declaration of war on relationships. In fact, genuine relationships stand on truth; anything other than truth destroys relationships.

Unfortunately, people often put themselves in uncomfortable situations, trying to help, to protect, to cover up, and end up being exposed to lies. Thus, finding a safe and peaceful ground may come with what is the truth. At the place where it is difficult to balance the truth with the lie comes the question of which place is safer. Especially in some places where recorders are secretly planted, the discovery of it alone can make anyone lie to cover the truth because of fear. This is often the life of an abused person trying to save what is believed to be saved, whether it is worth saving or not. I remember discovering such in every corner of my home, as confirmation that I was in a less safe place and might be in grave danger. It was time to stop pretending that something was fine when it was clearly not, or it was worth saving. This is called lying to oneself. A lie inflicted to the self in the belief that running away or separating ultimately may bring stigmatization; it may be true but worthy in such circumstances.

When deciding whether to keep a questionable relationship, ignoring gut feelings or hesitation about closeness can strain the relationship, but maintaining a measured distance may be a healthy and peaceful option. Being honest also exposes a state of vulnerability, and being vulnerable is necessary for a real relationship as it opens a dialogue that nurtures a healthy relationship. Even though vulnerability is often looked at as a weakness, vulnerability remains an important aspect of a genuine relationship. Sometimes, honestly seeking the truth can be a time-wasting exercise, because a person who does not try to admit wrongdoings when having a chance to do so, may be a dangerous person exposing a malicious intent. Seeking the truth demands a meaningful conversation even without expecting an admission but a much more plausible and comprehensive dialogue. Nevertheless pride may overshadow the admission of wrongdoings, and therefore, prevent a potential solution.

Also, falsehood can cloud the ability to make a thoughtful judgment to some degree, for having been repeatedly consumed with lies, people may become far removed from the truth and unable to understand what is true. Even a compulsive liar often inadvertently tells the truth but omits specific facts for self-protection or others. Imagine a situation where a kid says he is somewhere when he is not, only to convince loved ones not to worry about him. Or a teenager saying they did something they have not yet done to avoid punishment, only to have more time to procrastinate and play around. While doing so for self-protection, a priority should be not to hurt anyone else or create a pattern of lies.

Many issues with honesty come from the problems of being truthful with the self. We create scenarios to help cope with undesirable circumstances while giving ourselves reasons to be happy and avoiding whatever hurts. While that might be a helpful approach to coping with the lies, the approach can be damaging. Ignoring the bad that comes with them often becomes all that's considered. Assuming that lying is human nature and dealing with the facts as the norm and not fighting against it, it contributes to and facilitates a destructive social phenomenon. Because lying is more destructive than it is useful. It is hard to discern the truth without an even balance of facing the good and the bad.

Seeking truth should involve every aspect of our lives and the people around us, including in business, where people tend to seek maximum profits. And the question becomes about the quality of the products made. Nevertheless, it can be fascinating to witness a search for answers and the truth, in which breakthroughs or discoveries will solve a specific problem, not only a lie but something different. I refer to the fascinating television show, *Shark Tank*, which most are familiar with. Listening to the stories of entrepreneurs who set out to solve a problem by taking steps in the search for the accuracy of their formula, the potency of their product, or the efficiency of the service they want to create, that same exercise equates to a search for truth, a search for a certainty in the quality of the product, and thus, a certainty on the veracity of the information received.

Of course, we end up finding, learning, discovering, improving, and solving, etc. Those entrepreneurs do not only rely on the belief that their knowledge would help make a great product, but they also ensure all their questions are answered. They critically evaluate their knowledge and analyze the potency and usefulness of their product. Another dimension to how far the search for truth can play out. It can result in certainty, confidence, and peace of mind.

2
WHAT IS THE TRUTH?

"If you tell the truth, you don't have to remember anything."

– Mark Twain

The new notion of "my truth" that is often pushed to mask a lie is not really the truth, it simply means "in my opinion"; or "his truth," meaning "in his opinion." It may also mean what I think, or what he thinks. Frankly, it means a person's view or judgment formed about something, which may not be necessarily based on fact or knowledge of something, but also may have nothing to do with the absolute truth. The absolute truth focuses on what is the reality, on the fact of what is, or what actually happened. Speaking about "my truth" or "your truth" suggests that truth is relative to an individual, yet it is not. Truth is not relative. Philosophers often explain "truth relativism" by the fact that when someone makes a claim, it is made true or false by what they think or how they feel rather than by how the world is. Arageorgis provided such explanation in his *Relativism, translation, and the metaphysics of realism*. It suggests that the same thing or fact can be true for one person or group of people and false for another. Here, truth becomes dependent on the belief systems, independent of the facts. Unfortunately, many disputes often begin with the disagreements of what is true, and what is not.

"Absolute truth" may mean there can be no objection to it. For example, with "I exist," or "I am here," there is no doubt because I am here with no need to prove it. And that is the absolute truth. Anything contrary to it becomes a lie. "Your truth" is what you believe, and "the truth" has nothing to do with what you or anyone thinks or believes, but everything to do with the real facts.

The most difficult position for most people is choosing what to accept or believe, and facing mistakes, including lies. As human beings, people surely make mistakes. The thought that mistakes or faults could be disappointing and cause some kind of anxiety means making such mistakes becomes a defense mechanism. Think about the people who often paint themselves in a particular light that makes them appear different and more appealing. They make others think they are who they are not. For example, the phenomenon of *passing* in the African American community during the antebellum era is an illustration. *Passing* historically was referred to mixed-race Americans identifying as belonging to a different racial group, passing for white, to escape the legal and social conventions of racial segregation and discrimination, for example. Modern trans-sexuality, whereby an individual might pass into heterosexuality, to become who he or she is not, can be translated to modern-day passing, and all both notions have in common is a lie.

Our lives are marked with special events that may include dramatic ones, orchestrated by the goods, the bads, lies and false information. The information that paints a person's image with what he/she despises the most, with what he/she is not, to the point where the question whether life is about a lie or the truth, abounds. The Bible often gives us answers to any doubt. From childhood through teenage years, many people may have thought of lying as the practice of children or teenagers, as they lie to avoid the consequences of their actions, or lie to keep or break friendships, for example considering that friendship is the name of the game for the teenage experience.

Many grew up being taught to always tell the truth, to be honest and not lie, etc. Even one of the *Ten Commandments* says so. Growing up with the utmost example of honesty and integrity, to live in a society mixed with a bunch of evildoers, the madness of lies becomes evident. It is difficult to see how far lies can go in society and the world as a whole, so you must ask yourself: what is the meaning of truth? A society where it is easy and easier to get away with lies, in a world where, talking about a lie sounds like a taboo, a no-go area, but lies are prevalent, and they continue to cause extreme misfortune.

The truth is necessary to thrive. Truth is important. Believing what is untrue can impair plans and even cost lives. Telling what is untrue may result in legal and social problems and penalties, as discussed in another section. The concept of truth may have fallen on hard times, and the consequences of rejecting the truth ravages and ruins humans and society in general. Returning to the starting point, how would you answer the question: What is truth? The modern-day definition of truth can be very twisted but there is only one truth, and it is the truth.

An unbeliever posed one of the most profound and eternally significant questions in the Bible. Pilate, the man who handed Jesus over to be crucified, turned to Jesus in His final hour and asked, "What is truth?" It was a rhetorical question, a cynical response to what Jesus had just revealed: "I have come into the world to testify to the truth." Here it sounds more biblical than it sounds in real life.

Two thousand years later, the whole world breathes Pilate's cynicism, with different beliefs of what is the truth. Some say truth is a power play, a metanarrative constructed by the elite to control the ignorant masses. To others, truth is subjective, an individual world of preference and opinion. Many others believe truth is a collective judgment, the product of cultural consensus, and there is a faction that flatly denies the concept of truth altogether. And the question remains, what is truth?

This simple definition can be drawn from the Bible and translated to the real world: Truth is that which is consistent with God's mind, will, character, glory, and being. Even more to the point, Truth is God's self-expression. That is the biblical meaning of truth. Because the definition of truth flows from God, truth is *theological*. From the *ontological perspective*, truth is a fancy way of saying it is the way things are. Reality is what it is, because God declared and made it so. Therefore, God is the author, source, determiner, governor, arbiter, ultimate standard, and final judge of all truth.

Lying seems to be an art, the art of drying the truth, and a pathological liar fits the role. It tends to defy what is, and to profess what is not. Lying suits the state of a pathology when it becomes a habit, with the damage that ensues. What defines a pathological liar is his habit of unexplainable untruthfulness and his passion for lying, no matter the circumstances and the consequences. For a pathological liar, the consequences appear meaningless, as if destroying someone's peace and sanity with lies is their aspiration, and seeing others in despair and pain as a consequence may be to the delight of a pathological liar. A pathological liar suffers from a disease of repeatedly making up false information intentionally and with obsession. Whether he harms himself or others for doing so, whether he is aware of the consequences or not, nothing stops a pathological liar.

Very often, liars do not think that they could be harming themselves since their focus is mostly on others and on telling lies. They also do not believe they could be harming others or may believe others deserve the consequences of their lies and deceit. Unfortunately, what matters the most to pathological liars is the consequence, the result they want to see, and that is the goal they want to achieve.

Nevertheless, pathological liars tell lies that are often all-encompassing and convoluted, and the urge to tell them is incontrollable. As if lies are a tool to contradict, to cover up, or to gaslight. Pathological liars tend to undermine others' intelligence to understand their scheme. They are convinced that no one will pursue any research for the truth, and even though the truth is discovered eventually, pathological liars still deny, even though it may be too late. The danger in pathological lying is in knowingly making up stories without weighing the consequences. Lies can lead to various losses. It can be a loss of a position or of power, a loss of a relationship, a loss of favor, loss of opportunity, or can even cause a crisis one way or the other, and the list goes on.

Pathological liars genuinely do not believe in the importance of telling the truth, and even if they do, they may still think that it is the right thing to do in telling lies. What pathological liars and narcissists have in common is that their lying patterns come from a habit, an anti-social behavior, or borderline personality disorder. Regardless of the characteristics, the authors or reasons, lying hurts, and to be lied about is even more troublesome. Troublesome because people are glued into believing every word they hear without asking themselves, "Is it true?" And when they are able to pursue or face the truth, it might be too late and they can no longer be deterred from the lies.

Sometimes, showing a little doubt can sway the liar, but society is often asleep, believing without checking and then carrying everything on. And the culture has indulged the conditions and the motivation of pathological liars. They make it a passion to make up stories that sound real enough for people to believe them, and they feel very comfortable adding more lies to back up the original ones. Then the cycle continues. And the lies they tell become outlandish and easily disproved. It does not matter who lies, the effect is the same, and some famous people do too. They might falsely claim they were involved in a dangerous car chase in the middle of Manhattan during rush hour, where a chase is quite impossible, or at least has been proven impossible, yet many will still believe it to be true, just by hearing. Certainly, some do so to attract sympathy, and they get it, because many people are very blinded by their sense of compassion that they fall for every lie and never ask if it is true.

Those people can even claim that they are victims of some form of discrimination or racism, from the same people that held their hand, welcomed and let them into the circle, or opened an avenue for them. They use any prevalent form of lie as a weapon to get their way, yet many still believe in useful lies. They can even claim that they have developed a severe illness in the presence of a person they do not want to see, a person that they dislike, for example, and the majority of people will believe the claim and will never ask if it is true, yet people should.

While focus is placed on the benefits that lying brings only to the people making up the lies and causes losses to others, the attitude itself is selfish and is always about them and nothing else. Certainly, their action of lying changes the story, it distorts the truth, it sends false information, and even muddies the water to confuse the situation. Very often, they avoid having to take responsibility and accountability for the consequences of their actions, while claiming to be who they are not. These characteristics closely describe a mental disorder, a crisis a lie can cause, the price of their lying habit, the condition that influences their mental state and even life. There is probably no magic pill that can cure a pathological liar's condition. One may suggest not listening or believing anything a pathological liar may say, but only to pay no attention or reject the unverifiable lies. The way to avoid being caught up in such a circus is to be aware of the many 'telltale' signs that someone is not telling the truth or simply seeking attention as an important part of his well-being no matter how he gets it. It could be by blaming others, and that includes lying; thus, they make sure they achieve their goal.

When the time for recollection comes, everything that happened differs from the truth. And the story previously told becomes different. Then the distortion begins, adding to the manipulative scheme, not telling the truth, getting their story aligned becomes a challenge because a straight fabricated story cannot be managed. Nevertheless, keeping track of false stories and contradictions can be quite common but challenging, something liars do not do. They build lies upon other lies, and eventually lose track of them, relying on the lack of skepticism that they often encounter. Being skeptical can counter any scheme being played, and questioning anything we hear, however it is played, and not being swept away by the wind of lies. Especially considering what we hear to make any judgment or take position, doing so can help to avoid a crisis.

It is interesting that liars often target what the subject despises the most. They tell overly dramatic and dark lies of intense situations knowingly to intentionally hurt their victim, probably someone they despise and intentionally want to cause trouble for. Liars choose that dark and displeasing target to ensure they leave an impactful stain on the person's image with false stories and lies. Imagine being a person who deeply despises corruption, then someone who strongly hates you possibly comes to tell your community, your entourage, that you are corrupt. It may be something other than corruption, but the goal is to make you feel the pain of a deceptive lie, unless no one stays skeptical to question what they hear. This may sound familiar, because lying is a culture, and stories reciprocate.

Not only can the environment be pretty uncomfortable as a consequence, but being skeptical and having the ability to deter the lies means first holding the story in doubt and asking yourself if it is true, then moving to verify its accuracy and veracity if needed before making any judgment out of what is told. Not making a quick judgement may be wise; and making a quick judgment that can bring a position or a relationship to a halt for what has not been verified to be true is, on the other hand, unwise. Society has deepened into a sort of turmoil of lies, because no one questions what he/she hears. Such laxity is preyed upon by those who use lies as their weapons to build themselves up while destroying others. Of course, society would be a much better place if everyone could verify what they hear, but unfortunately, it is not always the case. Although it may not be very important to hold skepticism and demand research for truth unnecessarily, in the meantime it may not be important to make any judgment at that point. Of course, every story has two sides, a single story, and the other side of the story, which is no less important, as a way to counter lies of the single story, if any, and protect what is true. After all, the game of lies versus truth can be insane, but sanity comes first, and it may be recommended to hold firm and wait for the truth when playing such a game.

In reality, what is true is true; it is accurate, and no amount of lies can change the truth. But those who lie often think that repeating a lie over and over can make it become the truth. There is no question about how uncomfortable it can be for a person or situation to be lied to or lied about. Knowing what is true and hearing the lies being told consistently can make reality questionable, and make one question what the agenda could be. But whatever the agenda may be, telling or researching the truth is also an art, to disagree with and reject lies for the sake of peace.

The difficulty is being able to adjust to such an uncomfortable outlook, thus, trying to convince a different point to agree. But what matters is the truth. Unfortunately, the admission of being wrong becomes obsolete, because liars believe others are wrong, perhaps unintentionally. The bottom line is that the wrongs and the rights usually do not think the same way. They may just have different meanings of the same things or may have been reading different books or influenced by different types of people, and they also may have learned different theories. They may believe in different ideologies, meaning that the truth is a different reality from one group to another, which is a problem. Whether it is a lie or not, the difference in opinion is the name of the game.

If destroying others is the goal of the liars, at least in most cases, winning an argument no matter how, is another. Whether it is in a disagreement or just lying, it appears in a different light. Liars live in their own bubble of truth or reality, which is simply a mixture of truth and lies that they confuse as their way, what they need at any given moment. Whether it is for a business deal, a relationship dispute, a divorce proceeding, a custody dispute, a friendship, or even in politics, or other expected accomplishments that matter to them, no matter what it is, lying becomes the game, and liars play very well in these circumstances.

At the point where the act of lying shows no limits, interaction with others becomes limited, and setting boundaries becomes essential for self-health and sanity, because lies overwhelm. It does not matter whether others are pushed to tell the truth, or they are expected to have an epiphany; the tellers of lies do not change all of a sudden, they lie and get away with it and continue to do so. Although the goal is not to change the habit of lying, it would be good if it were, and to convince others of the truth and present the facts accurately on one hand, or to convince them of the benefit of not believing in the lies on the other hand, but to see the reality and seek the truth only. This can only be possible by making sure the truth prevails.

When lies motivate people to justify and rationalize their lies to themselves so any viewpoint can continue, they disengage from the situation and rationalize their thought processes to set themselves up to lie more in the future. Because they have found a way to justify their dishonesty. Therefore, the small initial lies escalate into other forms of dishonesty, making it more difficult to notice a slow erosion of integrity, moral code, beliefs, values, and principles. Then confusion grows in the process, lies become a culture, and shame vanishes from such behavior.

At such a stage, disengaging to avoid confrontations can help limit some interactions with a lying person. It is important to disengage from a conversation that does not benefit any good deed or instead turns to bitter disagreement. No one should have to force their opinion onto others, but liars are often very good at doing so. Sometimes, even the proof, the evidence of the facts, or the truth cannot be very convincing, because a pathological liar believes in his lies and has difficulty being convinced that they are lies.

As mentioned earlier, lying pathologically may be a sign of a bigger problem of any sort. When it reaches the state of a personality disorder, society as a whole may suffer. Consequently, badmouthing gains ground and often makes and encourages avoiding what or who has been the target of the lie, in other words, the victim. Certainly, the made-up stories and spread of disinformation increase and push into isolation, renunciation, and rejection as if it were the goal of such lies. Then, the victims find themselves in a defensive position, whether necessary or not, while the situation results in being portrayed by disinformation. Many of us have been in such a situation and for reasons difficult to explain.

3

THE BOUNDLESS MOTIVATION OF LIES

"The glory built upon a lie soon becomes a most unpleasant incumbrance. ... How easy it is to make people believe a lie, and how hard it is to undo that work again!"

– Autobiography of Mark Twain

The motivations behind the act of lying may seem complex and absurd, but they are not. Lies are often uttered inadvertently, but most of the time, they are made intentionally. In the modern world, lying has become fairly common, and getting away with lying may have made the act of lying the new norm. It may no longer be a shame to lie, though it should, because lying is immoral, and it can be criminal too. But isn't a lie supposed to be a taboo? It seems not, because the race to the top is a very complex one, and some racers have made the act of lying their way of racing, as if one may have to lie to get a pass, lie to be heard, to seek compassion, and even approval. Lying is often a tool to annihilate or destroy what a liar despises or does not want to see. The list goes on, graduating from the taboo to the norm. There is increasingly no shame in knowingly telling lies or making false statements, and increasingly no consequences in knowingly telling lies or making false statements; and society has slowly embraced such facts. While prominent cases of purported lies continue to dominate the conversation and even the news cycle, Christian Miller found that people tell more lies to friends and family members than to strangers. In his 2023 piece, *The Philosophy and Psychology of a Neglected Virtue,* he drew much greater attention to this neglected virtue, the art of lying. Such lies rarely end up in courts, although they can be criminal. What drives the increase in the phenomenon is the fact that not only does lying rarely end up in court, people rarely search for the truth but continue with the lies. Selfishness and a growing struggle for power and influence have taken over the culture, though people will go out of their way to acquire that sense of power, no matter what it takes, even if it takes lying to an extreme level, though the struggle for power may be personal as it may be collective. Then lies take the center stage.

Individuals, companies, organizations and even political leaders are at the forefront. They make less and less effort to fact-check their information. Whether it is the business release or political statement that guides their information, a simple fact-check or research may be helpful to uncover potential misrepresentations in case they exist. This may have become unnecessary, and false information may have become the information, a tool to deceive. Some products get recalled very often when the damage has already been done because no one questioned the quality of the product, though it can be difficult to do so, but worth doing.

Lies and false statements affect day-to-day lives. Information from companies that flood society with false advertisements, like politicians who lie in order to gain votes, portraying their opponent as a horrible candidate or making promises they know they cannot deliver. Thus, constituents believe those lies and fail to ask whether it is true. They fall for manipulative lies, only to vote against their own interest while politicians maintain power. Unfortunately, the people we care about, from relatives to friends, are no exception. And everyone is a perpetrator and a victim at the same time: Children who break a vase and swear they did not break anything, with the pieces scattered in front of them. Teenagers will say they are sick only to avoid doing their chores. In-laws will keep relatives on the outs then tell the world that these same relatives do not like them. A friend who can tell a lie about another friend, just to make sure the two are separated. A circle of lies that does not end. Acquaintances will come and go, calling you a bad person on the way out when they did not get their way, expressing some sort of frustration. If lying is not a tool at any level, why lie in the first place?

Giving false information is often intentional but happens to be unintentional at times. The fear of negative consequences may motivate the act, for protection from someone or something, to avoid an awkward or embarrassing situation, or for selfish reasons. While it may not be admirable, false statements often come in exceptional situations, with and without a clear purpose. The statement may not appear to the author to be false, making room for correction when determined to be, unless it is intentional. Nevertheless, in this modern world of communication, just like a lie, correction seems meaningless and unnecessary, as the damages may have already erased the necessity for correction, or the perpetrators remain adamant to their original position. Thus, in reality, there is always a reason and a motivation behind any lie, a reason that the person lying would not want that disclosure.

Countless reasons could be that:

- The person lying may believe the lie and what is said to be true.
- A person's memory may be unreliable.
- There may be pressure to say something to make a situation work or pressure for someone to do what is demanded for satisfaction.
- A lie may be what the person desperately wants to see accurate and make it true by repeating it over and over.

- A lie may be uttered to seek compassion, recognition and love.
- Because of the strong desire for power, influence and control, lying becomes a manipulation tool to push forth.
- When the truth does not match the desire, the person produces a lie to match those desires.
- There is a need to create a positive perception of the author because the truth may alienate someone or something.
- There is a need to create a negative perception of a despised person.

The list goes on…

Whatever the case may be, there is no legitimate reason to tell a lie. A lie is a lie, and the truth is the truth. It should be safe to believe everything that is said if a lie was really taboo, but we should be careful because it is not. Whether from a child standing in front of that broken vase and swearing that they did not do it, or from that politician standing at a podium, promising to do what they know they will not do. Of course, society has been taught to believe what they are told, and abuse has ensued with lies and deceit. Fortunately, that does not always happen; there is always room for skepticism, and therefore, it is important to dig deeper to determine if what has been said is true.

When lies are not questioned when they happen, and without realizing the effects, people's lives can change forever, maybe positively on one hand and negatively on the other hand from the same line of lies. Take the example of the best product advertisement, when relying on the ad and spending money to buy a product that is not good and can even jeopardize health. Whether the product was good or not, the best product statement alone is flattering. Yet questioning and verifying is another challenge that people live with. While they spend money to buy the product, the seller makes money in the end, and yet the health issue is evident. The seed oil controversy is an example, despite the claim being pronounced then debunked.

Imagine a lie that tells your entourage that you are a bad person, depending on what a bad person means. It may be unlikely that you are this discourteous and insolent person; it may mean that "I don't like that person, and therefore, nobody else should." Then, all of a sudden, your entourage stops waving hello, stops sending smiles, stops sending invites or even giving a helping hand occasionally, like they would ordinarily, and you end up paying the price because the collaboration and exchange are dead. Whatever the case may be, some lies put society in a lose-lose situation that only tears down, and no one wins except the liar who wins the pleasure to see the fruit of his lie.

Again, livelihoods can be destroyed because of false information. The experience of a lie may be hurtful if it cannot be righted. Even if it can be, it is difficult to erase the effect of a lie completely. Most of the time, making it right is only superficial. The example of a piece of paper is a lesson. When a piece of paper is mistakenly crumpled and thrown in the garbage, then picked back up because it is an important piece of paper that shouldn't be in the garbage to begin with, there is no way that piece of paper can be straightened out to its original shape, because it cannot, even under a hot iron. Taking the information from the paper may be useful, but the wrinkles remain in the paper. Same thing applies with a lie. A lie is a word that has power, and it sticks, even if we often hear "I take it back" when someone says something seriously inaccurate and wrong. Even an apology does not remediate a lie, although it is often called for. But it will depend on what was said and what effect it has had. The reality is that a lie has power.

What is it about lying? Despite being wrong, lying allows a person to establish a perceived control over a situation by manipulating it. It may be a defense mechanism that seemingly prevents people from being vulnerable, that is, from opening up and revealing their true selves to another person. It may also be an offense mechanism that people utilize to influence and manipulate others.

People who lie repeatedly often have that desire to be in control of a situation. When the truth does not align with such power and control, they produce a lie that conforms to the narrative they desire. In doing so, those people worry that the truth can leave them looking different from the person they want to be portrayed as. It does not matter if the lie ends up destroying others, for which destruction is sometimes their true desire. Of course, liars certainly trust in the ignorance or indolence of the listener to push their narrative. Ignorance because they do not know it is a lie, neither do they try to know, then lies go from one end to another, creating havoc along the way.

Take the case of in-laws who keep other in-laws at bay but tell the world that the latter doesn't like the first when the reality is that the first doesn't want to see the latter because they are now in a relationship through marriage. Marriage is a biblical institution that strengthens family relationships. For some, it is the beginning of one relationship and the end of another. Marriage may also be the end of siblinghood, where even lies have played the divider. The scenario resembles the case of a politician who tells his people that the opponent is a terrible candidate who will end the world should he win. Not critically thinking to assess the statement, people believe the lies and move on in fear, while nothing convinces them whether this may or may not be true.

Lying can be a tool to get back at people, or launched against a specific person for a specific reason, whether such a person has acted poorly or not. However, the lies told are intentional to destroy the targeted person. While a community may place the victim in some punishment mode like rejection, liars continue to play the good ones while ignoring and being insensitive to the hurt that the victim may suffer. Most of the time, the goal is to advance some individual agenda, whether to exclude the targeted person or make the targeted person the subject of hate, it certainly comes from a place of hate. In such a situation, not being skeptical is unknowingly facilitating hate or destruction. It is often difficult to contrast lies and destruction because while lies are audible and invisible, destruction may not be immediately understood, seen or felt, but the effect can be visible and devastating in the long run.

A friend of mine learned the effect of lies the hard way as a victim of how a single lie can bring your life, your entire family, to total destruction. Having been presumed to be guilty by the community before being found innocent by the court, my friend almost lost it all. He was held under solitary confinement because a student falsely accused him of inappropriate touching and more before the investigation proved him innocent. As a physical education instructor who is always ready and willing to assist any person in need, student or not, he found himself having to correct a student during his class. Sadly, the student complained to her parents and accused the instructor of 'sexual harassment.' To be sure the student truly understood the meaning of 'sexual harassment' she then described what happened, something different than reality, colored with lies. Why? Because the girl did not seem to like the instructor. The parents immediately pursued the case against the instructor. Never did they try to find out whether the allegations were true or false. Despite his denials of the situation, only the investigation and testimonies helped to find him innocent. Fortunately, the verdict of innocence cleared the instructor, but he could never return to his normal life. In the midst of such a storm, loss of freedom, loss of job, loss of money, loss of opportunities, loss of friends and relationships abound. And restoration hardly made him whole. The story may be familiar to many people reading this because our society has become so credulous to overturn the norms, but that is the society we live in. Next time, the question will be whether the allegations, the accusations, and what we hear are true.

Such a lie can even be adapted to a murder because in the midst of that storm, something died, inevitably and eventually, his lifestyle. His personality was attacked and has suffered. While you can see the manifestation of the murder even physically, lying is manifested in the invisible with strong words uttered into the universe, then travels through the conscience of the people who listen, then also manifests in the relationships that affect the victims. If a lie can cause a loss of a status or position, it can also cause the end of a relationship, the death of one's character that was the foundation of that relationship. It may also be that the lie has assassinated one's character and destroyed the relationship. What both lying and murder have in common is that they are wrongdoings and crimes, although sanctioned differently.

Sometimes lies kill relationships in many circles, whether a social circle or a family circle. In a family union, specially built upon love, trust and bond, circumstances may arise that could break the union, with a third-party addition through marriage. Of course, such an addition is a change in circumstances that often brings joy as well as turbulence. Without a transition period during which a relationship can strengthen its foundation, even at a personal and emotional level to facilitate the blending, a simple lie may easily break such a family union unless the foundation is strong enough to withhold the stream of such lies, eventually. But the lack of skepticism may only facilitate the breaking. In some cases, the effect of culture shock and personal emotions only exacerbates the matter. As a matter of fact, how many families have been broken as a result of such an addition? The ultimate truth is that a lie always plays a big role in such turmoil.

Since culture has turned easily into believing everything without question or not even daring to check the other side of the story, society has come to a shakedown of values. It is extremely baffling that in today's culture, people will consider false statements more easily, even about the obvious or a close person, than questioning the truthfulness of the words or information. Certainly, a lot of people have fallen victim because we live in a fallen society, so it would be much safer to question anything you and I hear before stating an opinion or making any judgment.

Often in school, students like to engage in competition. They compete with other students.

Everyone wants to be at the top, and some of them lie their way to the top. You may know what it is like when you get into a new school system, a system you are unfamiliar with, and you are assigned to group work. Very unpleasant at times, the experience was not pleasant for me when I was assigned to work with other students to simulate a contract negotiation with a client. Many great ideas and suggestions were discussed during the preparations to finalize our contract draft. Then, my partner, unknowingly to me, singularly met with the professor and claimed the ideas and suggestions were his. The professor acknowledged the ideas were terrific and evaluated my classmate at a very high level. Surprisingly, I discovered I could have been in a better position, had the professor considered my contribution, but I was not.

The situation put me in a position that disqualified me from many opportunities, until I met with the professor to discuss what could be done to remediate my situation, only to learn from him that I did not contribute to the group assignment. Surprised and confused, I reminded him that he congratulated my team for the ideas and suggestions. And to convince him, I went back to dig into communications that showed the original and initial suggestion. In fact, I made almost all the suggestions and ideas that supplemented our work, especially the one the professor praised the most. Forwarding my initial communications related to our assignment somehow convinced the professor of my contribution who then reevaluated my work.

Nevertheless, the changes came after many opportunities were already lost. Thus, a lie can go a long way you can never anticipate. Imagine being ineligible because of a small percentage of a point under the threshold. Then when every recourse is pursued and resolved, you find yourself above the threshold, thus you are eligible, but it is too late because someone lied. To go through such a process of claiming and explaining is often depressing and hurtful, but it is real. And to acknowledge that students could lie to take credit for the work of others is even resentful, given such mischief can disqualify one from opportunities.

The impact of using inaccurate information can be damaging in many ways; therefore, due diligence is important. In this situation of student competition, the professor assumed a private conversation to guide his evaluation without seeking to hear from the other students. Therefore, time was lost, pain was inflicted, opportunities were lost, and even friendships suffered. Nevertheless, it is very hard to catch up when you are trapped within a web of lies. Getting away with lies, while taking credit for others' effort and hard work, happens very often and does not make it normal and should not be acceptable. As a newcomer, I was also surprised that such naughtiness could happen in America, a place I thought was a perfect world, and that lying was something that only happened in a third world, but it is everywhere, thus, it was an eye-opening experience.

Indeed, something similar may have happened to the person reading this, not necessarily in school, even in the workplace. Then, when it happens and you choose to dispute, you may have to play on solid ground. Sometimes, some personal relationships, or even your last name, or your accent, may not be on your side. Most of the time, the people in charge of management, and even a professor in this case, do not always take the time for their own due diligence and rather rely on assistants. They may not ask questions to verify whether the information or the report is accurate and whether the information is true or not for consideration of what is presented or told to them. They rely on the assumption of competence of their assistant and trust to make a decision, neglecting a caveat where an assistant may deceive and lie. Not to vilify assistantship as a profession, but some bad apples do so about the people they despise, the people they want to see fail or leave. These unfortunate circumstances happen because society has become so conditioned and complacent in many ways. Having experienced such realities, one example after another, I understand how harmful and how devastating false statements or lies can be. How it terribly affects every area of our lives. It is important not to take information at face value, and it is important to always ask if it is true or accurate; thus, relying on lies to make judgments can be detrimental.

The message here is to be skeptical, meaning to look into authenticating and confirming the accuracy of any information we may want to use. Research for accuracy should not be measured up to confrontation in the case of what is told but to due diligence because it ensures the accuracy or truthfulness of the information. With true and accurate information, there are consequences too, and this can be devastating as well, but at that point, logic applies. Confrontation is never a solution, but if there is any doubt about the information, the action may not be necessary. Any decision has consequences, and the art of skepticism is to be able to hold back from making any decision until all the boxes of verification are checked to inform such a decision, no matter how it goes.

The effect of lying is also about giving consideration to what we hear, in addition to not getting the whole story or the other side of the story to find a balance and the truthfulness of what we are told. The effect of lying is about an internal dialogue that reflects the struggle of questioning the authenticity of information. The effect of lying is about doubt. Tame Impala, the popular psychedelic music project led by Kevin Parker, released their hit song "Is It True" as part of their album. It delved into themes of doubt, about love, and the complexities of relationships that are tainted with the untrue.

Diving deeper into the meaning behind this mesmerizing track, "Is It True," you find that it explores the doubts and insecurities that arise within a close relationship. The lyrics suggest a yearning for clarity and the need to know if the bond being experienced is genuine, and if it is true. This internal dialogue reflects the universal struggle of questioning the authenticity of what is told and the emotions surrounding it. It delves into the vulnerability and anxiety that often accompany the early stages of a relationship; being skeptical is the language. Everyone should be skeptical, not only in the early stage of a relationship, but about the unknown and about what we are told.

The lyrics encapsulate the turmoil and confusion that arises when trying to understand the depth of someone's feelings and understanding. It acknowledges the uncertainty that can cloud judgment and the desire for confirmation. The same should apply to the stories that people tell us, to the information we receive, and to what we are told. What informs a decision. Kevin Parker's vocals carry an earnestness that resonates with listeners, capturing the emotional journey of trying to decipher the truth when it comes to matters of the heart. While the song primarily explores love and its uncertainty, it also reflects on one's internal battles with self-doubt and the search for truth in another aspect of life. And if the search for truth is the right path for solution, seeking truth becomes conducive.

When taking information at face value, not knowing if it is accurate or not, you may want to think about the usefulness and the impact such information may have. Whether it is about a person or someone you know and love, you may want to think about the damage it may cause to that person. If it is about a project, you may want to ask yourself how accurate and helpful the information can be to advance the project. It is probably part of human nature that people lie, and that they invent stories to tell, good or bad, they give false information and make false allegations with sound or bad intentions. Whether it is to protect or destroy, whatever the case, there is always a purpose or an agenda behind the unfortunate lie. Information should not be taken at face value but should be used wisely.

Why Do People Lie?

Lying can be equated to disinformation: false information deliberately intended to mislead or manipulate vulnerable minds. We know by now that lying may benefit the perpetrator while destroying others, the victims. Still, many liars pretend to be the victims of some sort, only to manipulate and get others to believe their own disinformation or lies. The manipulation might involve getting others to join their crowd or make them believe they are in some fictitious battle, only to attract sympathy. Or the manipulation may manifest in creating more fear out of a specific situation than it should. Unaware of what they may be doing or getting themselves into, people believe everything they are told without questioning whether it is true because they want to be sympathetic to others; they easily believe in the lies but end up being manipulated.

When a lie is told in a form of a story, it may be about a third person or situation, yet there must be another version of that same story, and it may be wise to learn more and check the truthfulness of what is told:

- What is the other side of the story?
- Is it a true story?
- Is the information accurate?

What we are told is one thing; the question we ask should be another, and we should ask if what we are told is true. Unfortunately, culture has prepared and conditioned people to just listen and believe what they hear. Our culture has prepared and conditioned to "believe all women," the belief that has encouraged some women to lie or to revive old, unverified stories that are usually and unfortunately aimed at destroying someone's ascent, reputation, and career or someone they simply despise. What was called the "#MeToo" movement has pursued that path, unfortunately. As described by Wikileaks, it is a social movement and awareness campaign against sexual abuse, sexual harassment, and rape culture, in which people publicize their experiences in such. The movement draws attention to the magnitude of the problem and empowers those who have been victimized through empathy, solidarity, and strength in numbers. Women were supposed to be believed without being required to provide any proof of their allegation. Whether the allegations were true or not is still the question. Some were verified, and some, not much so. Even a highly televised hearing for the nomination of some high-profile personalities accused of sexual harassment did not result in any proof, while some entities [Hollywood] led a high-profile termination from positions because of the movement. Accusation was enough to terminate, and the question becomes: why should we believe without any proof, when we should be asking, is it true? Thus, the movement convinced the public to just believe women.

The world has become small thanks to the internet and the news media propagating information that may be true or false, yet the media's role is to lay out the facts. Election season too is interesting in the sense that it often becomes a season of accusations, sometimes with some strange, outdated stories. A season when someone's credibility has to be destroyed to make a case for another, whether the accusatory story is true or not. This tells us how disinformation, a lie, is often used to attack others, and it does not matter if it ends up destroying. Unfortunately, it works all the time because many will fall for what they hear, no matter what it is. And it takes a genius not to believe false stories that make headlines day in and day out because the headlines have to be front and center until the goal is reached. The #MeToo movement has contributed to playing such a role too, and the electoral propaganda in terms of campaign has done the same, in order to reach a certain goal while destroying others' credibility. When many women come out justly and unjustly to accuse someone of old, verified and somewhat unverified stories when the time is ripe, it never goes away. The example of the hearing for the nomination of a Supreme Court judge in 2018 taught us just that.

The rationale behind some false statements is often difficult to explain. Not only can we count the destructive intent behind the lies, one of the motivators is to avoid exposure or punishment, whether as an adult or a child. People may lie to protect themselves or others, to avoid embarrassing situations, to protect their privacy, or even to cause harm to others as lies always do. Because exposure often causes a loss of credibility, position or relationship, it may also cause a loss of freedom, opportunities or privilege, putting many lives in a different or dire situation. Surely, lies can build mountains as much as they can move them to destruction.

The rise of the #MeToo movement started out as a way for survivors of sexual assault, harassment, and bullying to share their stories, to bond together and support each other. Then, it evolved into a web of lies and sparked significant changes and conversations about the widespread issues surrounding them but ignited many controversies. Whether the stories of harassment or rape were true or not, it was and still is very difficult to fathom trying to verify them. Yet the strategy or movement worked because society was taught to "believe all women." That was the trend. The good news is that conversations around sexual abuse and harassment, with its ties to other systems of oppression, are still happening years after the movement began, as they were before. But this denotes how far a lie can go when no one asks, is it true?

Emotional Manipulation

Lying is an emotional exercise that creates a burden or load on others. It generates involuntary changes in behavior, making the listener question the person and not the statement. In other words, lying makes the listener question the liar and not the lie. A load starts with emotional manipulation by playing a victim to attract sympathy, and once sympathy is gained, it opens the gate to the web of lies. Such a series of lies where consequences do not matter as much may only continue to proliferate. Stories and lies are told flawlessly, with no chance of rejection or punishment. Surprisingly, a reward or even the crowning for having told a one-sided destroying story is that it is crowned by acquiescence and compliance. Unfortunately, we live in an era of confusion, where a lie is even rewarded, and a liar is treated as being courageous. For some, it's the courage to declare a new identity, to tell the world that he is who he is not, or she is not who she is, and sometimes just to take advantage of specific benefits or events, most often in sports too.

Even if the warning signs show that the allegations may be false, disinformation, lies, people will likely believe them and use them against others because this is the new culture, a culture where everything seems to be tainted with lies, and truth is overshadowed by the trend. The fact was already biblically introduced: The *"Ten Commandments"* instructed us not to bear false witness, to prepare us for deceitful human nature, even though not everyone believes in the

"*Ten Commandments*" or anything biblical. One of the commandments explicitly states that "You shall not give false testimony against your neighbor," another way of saying that you shall not lie; but people do. Although many do not believe in anything biblical, modern civilization was founded on those biblical principles, thus we swear on the Bible.

Disinformation is usually deployed to conceal any benefit or reward the person pushing the disinformation might receive. It makes people think of one thing when it might be another. Disinformation is false information that breaks a rule or apparent hope or expectation. Imagine a person who claims a network disruption when expected to be reached; it may not seem like avoiding a call, but there was a call and no return. Also think of a teenager who, desperately wanting to spend more time with friends, may instead figure out a lie as an excuse and will make sure to send out false information. Interacting with law enforcement can be interesting too, not a good place for presenting false information, where it is not appropriate to lie. At a check point, lying may be a rationalization as an excuse for any violation or any reason to justify the violation. In any case, the excuse is always already figured out before breaking a rule just in case they are caught. The bottom line is do not lie; being honest and telling the truth can even inspire your being excused in this situation.

Remember, the intention of a liar is not to come out as a liar but as a victim or an honest person. And the person lying usually succeeds and never gets questioned about their excuse or false statement, thus the lie plays emotionally into anyone involved, with one providing compassion to the other, and no one questions the truthfulness of any statement. However, people lie to avoid negative consequences. They also lie to distort the truth or to undermine others. Lying may make people feel good in a complicated situation, yet it is often rewarded somehow, depending on the side each person stands on. The reward comes in the form of being considered to make a decision without exercising the discipline of verification. Imagine a person lying to seek validation, to be included and even to seek favor and actually get it. It appears this plays out very well in the social media world for potential social presence.

Also, when lying protects others from harm, which is possible, people do, and we may say that the protection from one end may cause destruction on the other. While the same lie protects one, it may also expose or destroy another. Whether there is any justification for telling a lie, telling the truth can keep it simple and peaceful, because a lie will always bring controversy no matter the reason. We see situations where people may refuse to testify against a fellow because they do not want to tell the truth to make things worse for this person, and they do not want to lie either, even though they know this person behaved inappropriately or broke the law. Thus, silence becomes better than a lie. In an investigative situation, refraining from testifying should be motivated and commanded. While no one wants to appear as a 'snitch' or 'fink,' the use of anonymous call-in lines has proliferated. It encourages voluntary calls with useful information, and it avoids the danger of providing truthful information with a risk of being exposed, because retaliation may ensue.

Imagine a person in an abusive relationship, constantly lying to protect the abuser, because fear has overshadowed the ability to tell the truth, but unbeknown to oneself, the situation plays into self-destruction until help comes. In most situations, people tell lies to protect themselves and become truthful only when they are in a safe place; but no matter what the situation, the safety of the person matters the most as much as the truth.

It is important to protect oneself or others, and it is also important to weigh the consequences of lies, especially the ones that destroy. In some circumstances, whether by breaking the rules, making false statements, protection may be the priority. Take an example of a child opening a door to a stranger; it is a situation where the child might say something untrue, either to protect their home or their parents. If the child says there is no money in the house when there is, or their parents are home when they are not, or their parents are home but do not want to be disturbed, the child's actions may be a lie but protective. The child intelligently sought to protect his family with a false statement. Thus, the conversation displayed a confidence in the child to measure a useful lie.

Children, too, understand the difference between the truth and a lie, the ability to tell the truth and the necessity to tell a lie. Children, too, can protect the privacy of their family and keep secrets even if they need to lie to do so. However, a challenge for parents is how to keep their children safe because they understand their ability to manipulate the truth and lies and may not be telling them the truth either when it comes to what is happening in their lives. Because children like the attention of their peers, they often boast about something untrue to win sympathy, friendships, or admiration. And some adults do the same, playing the game of lies that can do more harm than good, mainly embarrassing and damaging in the end. Yet the habit of lying and the power that comes with it, over a targeted audience, seem to be rewarding instead because lying often goes unquestioned and unpunished. The situation of the child lying to protect his family is only an exception.

Eluding embarrassing situations is another motive for even the most trivial of lies. When a child wets the bed and says he spilled a glass of water on the bedding or his clothing, he wants to avoid punishment, and most of the time, it works. Then the child matures with the habit of lying and employs the scheme when necessary and useful. Embarrassment might be a path to resolving some covered issue, while honesty can bring forth the courage to find and openly seek solutions that come with telling the truth. And lying has made headway because it is not openly challenged and rejected at times, and when it is not, it goes on. As long as a lie is not a source that spells danger, some can be overlooked if they do not quite affect anyone's being. Of course, not every lie calls for a need to be challenged and rejected; it may not be necessary or worthy of attention, but simply be ignored. While the situation of the child lying to protect his family is an example, the situation of the child who wets the bed and lies about a spilled glass of water is not because it needs to be remedied.

However, some efforts to be polite may be commonly as deceptive as a lie. Such as comments of fake appreciation of something when we do not really mean it, but the person receiving the comment often believes it; in other words, a deceitful form of praise. Comments like "I like your dress" or "you look good" are frequent comments that are often more flattering than true, yet people want to hear more because they like to be told what they want to hear. The ability to question what we hear can also prepare us to receive and manage whatever compliments we receive and the lies that come with them, because we live in a fallen society filled with lies, where the courteous and fake compliments or the naked truth are prevalent. And surprisingly, some may prefer to be lied to and not be told the truth that they want to hear, like telling a lady that she has gained a few pounds extra, but no, that would be "rude" even if it is true. This is the kind of truth that a lady would not like to hear, yet we are to always ask if what we hear is true; so when we find the truth, we should accept it and deal with what it comes with, because anything contrary is a lie.

Lies without Boundaries
We live in a culture of lies because society has lost its way; open minds and critical thinking have withered away or have been undermined. Ignoring subtle clues or suspicious behaviors to avoid facing the harsh consequences if the truth is discovered, swearing becomes a way of telling the truth or justifying a lie, then it becomes more comforting to believe the lies. The odds are that when a person has been lied to, or lied about, the person becomes skeptical, and seeking the truth becomes one priority. To address the question – why do people lie? For a number of reasons. Dan Ariely, a behavioral psychologist at Duke University, once said, "the dangerous thing about lying is people don't understand how the act of lying changes others." Seeking to understand why most people lie often results in the findings that those with the lying disorder impulsively lie for no apparent reason, or every reason possible, and some of the most common motivators are pro-social and altruistic reasons powered in the race for control. And most who lie do not often know why, some do not even know that they lie, and for many, it is simply a pathological disorder.

Sometimes, lying is a fun activity. Telling children about Santa Claus being real may be considered pro-social, while it makes Christmas an exceptional experience for children, who happily believe in it, no questions asked as long as the Christmas presents arrive. Lying means hiding what does not need to be known, or changing what should be known, in an effort to hide what is true. Although some truths may be hurtful, not telling someone the truth for fear of hurting others may be altruistic, often a way to show care. A caring tactic like the Santa Claus scheme may fit the category.

No matter the situation, telling others the truth should not be understood as exposing anything or being vulnerable. It is always better to deal with the consequences of the truth once and for all and seek remedy, than to deal with what may seem to be the shame that may come with exposing the truth. This perception perhaps contributes to the perversion of the culture. People do lie to hide the truth. If the truth may appear as exposing something, and lying becomes acceptable, why not only focus on doing good so that telling the truth does not appear as exposing or as treason but an expression of reality? That would make life easier, better, and peaceful too. When it comes to compulsive liars, they tend to lie about everything and consistently to get their way because they fear the truth will not get them what they want. For example, lying for the reasons of association and inclusion with others where they long to be acknowledged and validated is only a glimpse of the reasons. Compulsive liars fit in almost every category of liars, making lies become habitual and descriptive of the culture, much like a sociopath.

Sociopaths do lie repeatedly, and to make matters worse, they also:

- Develop a lack of empathy for others they are lying to or about.
- Have no remorse for the lies they have pushed or anything they have done.
- Have disregard for others.
- Often have poor interpersonal relations.
- Become professionals at manipulating.
- Are skilled at portraying a character or image they do not have.
- Pursue character assassination of others.
- Focus on destroying the person they despise through misrepresentations and lies.

Those are some of the characteristics and symptoms of most sociopathic liars, though we live in the midst of it every day and suffer the consequences.

Sociopaths, people with personality disorders, are openly willing to act illegally and they fail to conform to social norms. Their repeated intentional lies sometimes lead to misrepresentation, false statements, and deceit. Conning others for personal satisfaction, profit, or the simple pleasure of it are only a few examples of the sociopath's characteristics that negatively affect the social environment. Unfortunately, these characters exhibit aggressive behavior, irritability, rejection, disrespect, and a reckless disregard for the well-being or the safety of others. Lying is a dominant attribute of a sociopath, anything including being irresponsible consistently and not sustaining consistent behavior, an attribute that when multiplied, can slowly destroy society.

Sociopaths are indifferent to and rationalize mistreating or hurting others as a normal behavior. They are somehow insensitive, heartless, inconsiderate, and also, sadly, find some pleasure in lying and manipulating the people around them into thinking a certain way. Their irrational behavior often takes them to the point where they become addicted to their habit of lying. Also, they misrepresent to anticipate and avoid the angry outbursts, criticism, or judgment that may come from the reactions to their actions, except they will not put themselves in others' position when the tables are turned; they just do not think about the other side.

Sociopaths find pleasure in lying; no matter how destructive their actions may be, they continue to lie. Breaking such a habit may temporarily solve the antagonistic and hostile environment with a sociopath. In doing so, engaging in a conversation may be meaningful. Yet, the difficulty is that sociopaths are never prepared and do not welcome any conversation; instead, sociopaths tend to dictate.

The Agenda of Lying

Some make lying a way to achieve an agenda, a hidden goal, while telling others to look away; they make their way while breaking others' way, often by painting a positive image of themselves and a negative image of others. Let us think about this. When I consider the size of my current entourage, I realize it has shrunk. At least it is more peaceful now. It has shrunk because the crowd of lies has taken over a portion of it, namely those who follow without asking if what they are told is true. Yet they follow the crowd, blindly. Following a crowd must be a fun exercise, as it is the trend, except the end is unknown.

Let us talk about guilt by association, to despise in association with the person telling a lie, to push others to join a group of people who simply despise others because they have been invited by a lie to do so. Yet they despise someone they do not know, simply by associating themselves with a person who despises someone else. Liars do so because they want the person they despise to be rejected or judged based on their lies, so they damage their reputation or image at any cost. And it works every time because society seems to have forgotten its role to teach how to question everything or to never trust everything.

Although no one wants to be lied to, people are lied to all the time and are not always aware of it. And yet it becomes a culture. The caveat of just believing in the things we hear creates a vacuum of lies, whereby everyone, anytime spurts a lie and gets away with it. Of course, it is no one's responsibility to make anyone honest or truthful, or stop someone from concocting lies, but questioning what we hear and contributing to develop and cultivate more honesty and trust in our environment is everyone's responsibility. And how do we do that? When we nurture a mindset of honesty and cultivate a character of truthfulness, by always asking, is it true?

4

LYING SHALL BE ILLEGAL

"Therefore, the spoken lie is of no consequence, and it is not worthwhile to go around fussing about it and trying to believe that it is an important matter. The silent colossal National Lie that is the support ... of all the tyrannies and shams and inequalities and unfairness that afflict the peoples - that is the one to throw bricks and sermons at."

–"My First Lie and How I Got Out of It"
by Mark Twain

Mark Twain's comment derived from the observation that one can get away with lies without consequences, no matter the damage they cause to others on the way. Tyranny, inequality, and unfairness are just some of those damages. In most day-to-day circumstances, people can be whoever they want to be; some choose to be two-faced, disloyal, unfaithful, misleading, or deceptive, as long as it brings benefits and no punishment to them, it becomes part of the culture.

A culture of lies, where truth is a luxury, where anyone can say anything and even call someone a criminal or a monster without having to show any proof, they make it up, and it becomes someone else's identity. The made-up adjective can taint someone's identity but only if it is told to someone who believes without question. By not asking the question whether what they are told is true, they make themselves available to follow a crowd for a cause they know little about. All is needed is a lie, often uttered under protected speech. When the freedom to speak goes as far as leading to something sinister, the question of the lawfulness of the statement unfolds.

Although the broad latitude of expression has its limitations, in most situations, when the government is involved, it is precluded from charging someone for lying under the lens of the law. However, lying can have one brought to justice very fast. Whether it is deliberate or omission, a person can sue or be sued if the lie results in damages of some sort to others, because a lie is not that free even though speech is free; therefore, do not lie, that is the best advice. Telling the truth and checking the truth heals the culture of lies. Lies may not be used to accuse and condemn, to protect or destroy. The truth is uncovered eventually. While it can be uncomfortable for someone to defend against lies, life can get tangled in a situation of guilt by association because someone tells a lie and convinces everyone to run with it. Life can get intricate when the lies are uncovered, and a person telling the lies loses all credibility. There is no triumphant outcome. The only triumph is the truth and the ability to tell the truth no matter the circumstances, the ability to be skeptical, and the ability to check the other side of the story before making any judgment. The ability to ask yourself: Is it true?

As a matter of course, freedom of speech gives people a broad latitude to speak freely, and that shall not be infringed. Unless the speech promotes obscenity and lawlessness, free speech is constitutionally protected in the US as much as it is in the freest countries of the world. The latitude of this makes people think they are free to say anything and in any circumstances. But not when it conflicts with other legal protections. Though people have freedom of speech, it is not to be confused with the freedom to lie. Lying when you are not legally allowed to say what appears to be a lie can have dire consequences, leading to being fined or imprisonment. While laws may vary from jurisdiction to jurisdiction, from country to country, lying in the circumstances that qualify the action as a crime is not advised, though no lie is. There is always the possibility of an exception to the rule in any situation. Although our broad latitude to express ourselves is legal, lying is generally illegal. But let us not get deep into the law. No one has to be guilty of an underlying crime or has to be under oath to be forced to tell the truth, because the truth protects. In fact, one may not realize that there could be an undercover agent anywhere, ready to catch lies, anywhere, anytime. And some casual conversation can be overheard, recorded, and may go a long way if it shields a lie. The habit of telling what is true can protect and save, and no one will have to worry about breaking the law in such circumstances.

Some conversations may appear as jokes, as people do at times, but circumstances of conviction come under some jokes that shield lies, or under the law for lying while under investigation. Someone may be at the wrong place at the wrong time with a lie, but the truth protects at anytime and anywhere. Some famous figures learned such the hard way and were taken down for what they had said. We may remember the cases of George Papadopoulos, Martha Stewart, and Scooter Libby, who were all accused of lying deliberately, a perfect example of how lying can get people into trouble when freedom of speech is not there to protect.

For those who are familiar with the court of law, the statement that comes very often, "the truth, the whole truth and nothing but the truth" implies that you should not lie, or you are in trouble. Making any possible effort not to lie is fundamental in a courtroom because truth is the epitome of justice. This applies outside the courtroom as well, in circumstances where lying becomes a crime, and worse if done under oath or in a written statement.

Lying under oath or in a written affidavit may be raised to the level of perjury, or in other words, intentional lies. The court of law is the embodiment of the law as well as the truth, yet people often succeed in evading it. Unfortunately, today is a different time, and lies are often caught even in that body. Because the courtroom is the embodiment of justice, people are presumed innocent until proven guilty, meaning that not only shall everyone have a chance to be heard, but also that everyone must be presumed innocent until the court can decide otherwise after hearing and reviewing all the facts and evidence.

In making a decision, the court often listens to all parties involved in the matter and makes a judgment based on all the facts, hearing and seeing the evidence presented. Translation: the judge may hear both sides of the argument before deciding on the innocence or the guilt. This should apply to society as a whole. But in modern days, it appears that people are presumed guilty until proven innocent instead because society easily runs with one side of the story and even condemns the other side based on a one-sided story. A single story is a problem. Very often in circumstances where lies trump the truth, anything people say is believed by others to be true without verification. Thus, complacency with lies replaces attention paid in not taking what is told at face value.

Sadly, critical thinking is slowly disappearing, even in education. Students become followers of popular ideology, and also of lies, lacking the care to check what is true and what is not. Most people follow the crowd without prioritizing logic. Cutting and pasting becomes not necessarily a problem, but the new trend, yet knowing where to cut and where to paste also becomes a challenge. The same thing applies to information received. Due diligence matters and thinking critically matters as well. It begins with checking the information for accuracy, it begins with the question, is it true? Critical thinking is encouraged and rightfully so; it goes beyond just thinking clearly to practicing well-thought-out thinking for the decisions that we make about anything we do. It helps to decipher the information we receive. Thus, thinking critically improves when people do not simply believe and follow, but when they ask themselves, it is true?

One phenomenon observed in society is facing law enforcement, which is usually a very scary experience for many. It feels like facing reality. Facing law enforcement means you have to respond for your actions according to the law, your obligations and your rights too. Most often, the thought of getting a ticket and paying fines or being arrested when confronted by law enforcement tends to make people lie to get away with their wrongdoings. Lying to law enforcement alone can lead to being prosecuted, whether the person was involved in a crime or not. Lying alone can be considered a crime in certain circumstances, and lying in such situations can make encounters with law enforcement very chaotic.

An encounter with the law enforcement can happen unexpectedly, at any time, and there is no need to or good coming from a lie, even to protect. Generally, everyone should comply with law enforcement, but no one is under any obligation to offer help to law enforcement in case of investigations, other than providing identification when required. If someone decides to do so, it is better not to offer any information than having to think about what to say and lying; this is the worst scenario. It may be smart to remain silent. The damages of false statements or false accusations can take the parties down an undesirable rabbit hole in many ways, as it does not stop with law enforcement. It has a domino effect in other areas as well.

Some view lying as a way to reduce their risk, and it becomes a social currency embraced by those who seek to benefit the most from a person or business misrepresentation. Perhaps the motivation behind the making of false statements becomes the maximization of gain with lying as a tool. No matter how deeply lying has permeated society, this area is a red flag; lying to gain anything is fraud, and lying in business is destructive. And in general, liars know how to lie and how to prepare their defense. Liars prepare their defense with short facts and situations that they can twist, change, mis-define, and misinterpret in their favor, adding more lies to other lies.

In the advertising world, as mentioned earlier, advertisements are a witness of how lying is inscribed in culture. Most advertisements have something misleading, and it has one mission, to make a gain, even if it means lying to the public or destroying the competition in the process; lying in advertisement helps achieve that mission. Companies, businesses, politicians, and individuals often provide misleading or inaccurate information in their advertisement's skit, even though it violates some legal principles. Although it may be prohibited, advertisers are confident they can get away with their misrepresentation of the nature and quality of their products. They have studied the law and learned how to protect themselves in their manipulation, and they frame their skits carefully. Also, they rely on the complacency of people and society as a whole, and also on the fact that it might be costly to pursue them legally.

Even more, advertisers rely on the fact that the vast majority will never fact-check or question anything because lies have tainted the culture at all levels; thus, people believe anything they hear. And advertisers have considerable leeway in making statements, such as the best of everything, on their labels to attract sales. Although these are not prohibited, nothing indicates that they are true. Because the best of everything is a fact which accuracy cannot be proven; it is up to the buyers to make their own judgment. Thus, they will believe anything they hear and make purchases based on false advertisements because reading the label might not be a priority for many people, which it should be. In the end, buying a product wrongly advertised might jeopardize your health while the advertiser makes a profit.

5
AN AFFLICTION TO SOCIETY

"A lie is like a cancer that's spread to every single area of our lives."

– Simone Elkeles

In the prevalence of lies, the gullibility of the people cannot be underestimated. The question, is it true? Becomes like too much to ask. Liars are motivated by the belief that their listeners will believe without questioning what they hear. The most significant issues in society include misinformation, disinformation, lies, and any problem with the truth. People often take any information at face value and believe in anything they hear, and liars use that void to spread even more. Why wouldn't they? If they know they will not be believed at face value or what they say will be questioned, of course, they will not take that route, and they will not lie. And that would be one less problem.

Imagine telling someone what the person wants to hear; the person will certainly believe that what they hear is true. It is just that simple. Imagine complimenting someone's ugly hat, or someone's tasteless casserole as delicious, when in fact the hat is not very nice, and no one liked or ate the casserole. It is called a compliment, a polite expression of praise. It also sounds like a white lie, usually understood as something mundane or trivial that may not be considered damaging but can turn into the worst case of appreciation or humiliation when it multiplies. White lies are a hot topic; they are small scale, bottom level lies that are simply entertaining.

Lies are a form of malady to society, the wrong way of communicating a message and the worst way of finding a solution to any problem. Even as simple as saying to a friend or someone that the food they made for the party was delicious when, in fact, it was terrible; could this be harmful? Probably not. It can be encouraging to hear that food is good; it makes the person want to do more or even better, unless it puts their health at risk. After all, it may be best to keep quiet because the issue is not the food but the lying, and it is deceiving to do so. So why lie in the first place? Because lying has filled the culture. It has become a habit as if it is of value. Say something to be part of something, make up something and say it to be valued. It may be much better if it is something truthful.

In the political world, a politician or their agent can make some headlines with something as simple as a lie told on behalf of an authority to the public, or simply any lie. As a result, the news media would take on the story and run with it worldwide. This may sound familiar watching the media that often runs with information, misinformation, and disinformation without peer reviews or fact-checking. How many times have we heard lies, even in the higher sphere of society? At the level we were taught to be highly ethical, where everyone swears to tell the truth and nothing but the truth? Yet it often confuses the public with what is true and what is not, or it is true one day and false the next, and information becomes a web of lies full of misinformation and disinformation with no clear definition. A web in which every truth becomes a conspiracy theory, and a lie becomes the truth. Examples can be controversial too, and yet paying close attention to what is conspiracy theory may lead to the truth over time. The recent pandemic was life lesson, a crisis that took the lives of millions, because not enough truth was told or the public was not warned of the danger; no preparedness and adequate protection, and the damage was massive.

Sadly, society has welcomed and integrated the bad habits of being very comfortable telling the 'untruth' and getting away with it unchecked. Ethical behavior, integrity, and honesty require telling the truth even when it is difficult and uncomfortable. If anyone can handle a lie, anyone can handle the truth. Even science shows that telling trivial lies desensitizes the part of the brain that promotes uneasy feelings. That is true. Lying is sickening and makes everyone around sick, and lies damage reputations, relationships, and destroy personalities.

As mentioned earlier, white lies can turn from small into big ones very fast, taking on a life of their own. A lie starts, and it goes around, then it changes, then it comes back differently and creates a story in the process. However, being truthful and respectful of others' views is kind, and abstaining from being honest is unlike telling an outright lie. It is necessary for a situation such as giving thanks for a bad gift, and in any circumstance, gratitude can be offered with some degree of honesty.

Most of the time, white lies are harmless or justifiable because of their low stakes, and while they may not carry the same weight as a significant destructive lie, they do add up to have a negative effect on a person over time. For example, lying to conceal a secret gives it much more power and weight, while a white lie always grows to be more important; it may cause a rift in relationships or become more real. When it is repeated constantly, it goes around and never ends. The effect can transform a white lie into something all-consuming and uncomfortable, taking a toll on the mental state of the people involved and negatively affecting our culture. It often translates how sick a culture is, when it is so prevalent to lie about everything and everyone.

The bottom line is, being truthful feels good and allows people to be more authentic. Even though society seems to have integrated lying into the culture, not only does it affect people emotionally, but it is also exhausting. Unfortunately, lying becomes something that is expected or normal. The problem with white lies is that they often appear as unimportant, not a big deal, but when they become a way to cover up something else or a more profound truth, the real issues grow, and society begins to suffer the consequences. Instead of looking to promote honesty, the culture normalizes lies. Just like any unpunished wrongdoings multiply such wrongdoings, society normalizes the lies by simply believing anything, and it creates more lies, then people get away with them more.

A white lie is understood to be something mundane or trivial. Telling such a lie only to share feelings does also affect relationships, but not always in a good way. It alienates others from closer relationships with peers, friends, or relatives, and the consequences can be much worse than imagined. Lies have these negative effects, such that they can be unbelievably destructive and divisive, as has been proven. Most people have already been victims of such, maybe not new, but what lesson have they learned from the experience? Liars use the same tactic every time and cover it; they alienate and destroy at the same time with lies, especially when the victim is not aware.

However, once the victim knows the scheme, the tables can turn one way or another, and the victim often takes a leave with distance. Taking leave may be the best way to cope with the weight and anger that lies bring; and it is much easier and more peaceful than remaining in an insane atmosphere of lies. Some may try to correct the record as a strategy for all concerned, be it with confrontation, questioning, explanation, or clarification, which could create more debility and weariness. Correcting the record is often unnecessary in the absence of a negative impact for the sake of an apology. Liars rarely apologize or admit to any wrongdoing, and they keep on going, doubling down and making the case for why friendlessness and shielding often make sense.

At a shielding stage, trust becomes an issue; we lose trust in everything and in everyone because every resource has been exhausted. Every attempt at making peace has been exhausted. Trust is lost with realizing how far people can go to create damage or destroy what they want to destroy with lies. And isolation becomes a place of peace when it comes to a person, a place that allows the person to live with an inner self knowing that there is only one truth, which is the truth. For these reasons, everything else does not matter. Being alone also leads to a feeling of uniqueness and questioning of others' thought processes.

One factor that plays in the scheme of lies is honesty, a moral correctness that entails showing respect toward others. Honesty about wants and likes is important. And the most important thing is to have the type of people who can positively affect the lives of others, treat them the way they want to be treated and get the same treatment in return, the people who value their peers and do not carry lies around. Honesty is a characteristic of great value and good type. Honesty is free of lies; it is difficult to understand or easy to be misunderstood as a victim of disinformation, because common sense is lost, as well as a sense of critical thinking.

When a society embraces a culture of lying as human nature and integrates it as a norm, how does it affect the values? What does it say about society when it rewards lies and liars? What does it say about society as a whole? Understanding the victims of lies and finding it harder to walk in their shoes can be a brain exercise. The challenge of isolation or seclusion may give others an impression of what a victim may endure. Not only does it affect the victim one way or the other, but isolation also affects those around a victim, their family, friends, or colleagues; for that matter, it affects the liars in return. And the impact of lies goes full circle and touches everyone around.

Is It True?

This is a simple question that may make society a much better and more peaceful place. There is no doubt society will be much better if people ask themselves that first question when they hear anything, a story about a situation or a person. Of course, lying may happen, and it happens constantly, but it should not be normalized, nor must one side of the story be considered, a single story, or even use a single story to make a judgment. Chimamanda Ngozi said it best in her *"The Danger of a Single Story,"* a story that only presents one perspective, repeated over and over, showing how it can be offensive and misleading. She believes that single stories can have a malicious intent to suppress other perspectives, or other groups of people, because the story may not be true, and there is no evidence to the contrary. If the story is invalid, it would be easy to make a wrong judgment, not only about the person telling a lie but also about the person the story or lie is about. The victim could suffer morally or mentally as a result, and the pain could be irreversible. The danger of suffering morally or mentally is that no one sees the danger; it is invisible and internal. Because no one sees it, people do not think pain exists, so the scheme continues and renews, and the pain grows. And a single story may negatively impact society when people judge, condemn, and reject based on that single story. Yet there is no effort to cast doubt on the story and seek the other side. Unfortunately, no question is asked as to whether it is true.

Many decisions made as individuals and as a society depend on the information received and on how accurate the information is. However, psychological biases and predispositions make people vulnerable to falsehoods. As a result, misinformation becomes more likely to be believed and remembered. Although the bad information can be later recalled after its falsehood unfolds, it may have already done its damage. Thus, it is difficult to erase something that the brain has registered, or there may still be room for adjustment and, therefore, correction.

The belief in something or someone without question is not unusual, even when there may be substantial proof that people are being lied to; that is the new norm. Bringing evidence to anything becomes somehow harder to overturning a line of lies. It requires tact and patience simply to persuade and convince anyone of the truth and to counter the lies. Of course, the exercise may only be necessary in the face of a very important matter when attempting to reconcile what is believed to be the truth with lies. When it is difficult to tell whether we are listening to the truth or lies, we often automatically believe we are being told the truth, and everything becomes the truth, including the lies. It is sad and painful when it involves someone or something we care about; then, the pain becomes even greater and worse when the person is someone close.

In the era of misinformation and disinformation such as this, we are surrounded with and absorbed by lies. While the media plays its role, the first thing that comes to mind is that the information is true. News media has been the source of information forever, and no one could have thought that lies could be part of it. Growing up, who did not run to the television, grab a newspaper, or listen to the radio in the quest for news and information? Because of the belief and conviction that they have done due diligence, peer review, to present what is accurate, as they should. When the same news media take society's reliance for granted, they inject any information they see as useful for their program, whatever they want the public to hear, including lies. Still, society can handle lies and still run to such sources for information. Sadly, society has taken such a direction, embracing lies as the new norms. And when the truth is discovered, correction is hardly ever made. Because it appears that the public cares less about the truth. Does it make any difference? Although it should, lies have permeated culture and confused the truth, and it becomes difficult, timely and often costly to differentiate the two.

Some corrections often come in a lengthy investigation, or in the form of explaining the reason for the lies; that is where the "my truth" or "his truth" come as if there are many truths. There is only one truth about a specific fact: "the truth." It would not be advisable to go over enumerating the lies from such news media. Their role is to inform the public with the truth and accurate information and not deliberately lie. I can remember the "Russia" election scheme that shook politics and became the subject of the news for years, then happened to be very false and slanderous. In fact, after the surprising 2016 election outcome in the United States, the unexpected winner was accused of having colluded with a foreign country to win the election. The media ran the news story for years, and many Americans were convinced that they had a foreign agent in power. After years of investigation, there was no evidence that sustained such allegations of collusion. The American Bar Association also published the outcome of the investigation. Then the news media moved on, as if nothing had happened.

No justification, no explanation, no correction. Surely reputations were destroyed, millions were spent unnecessarily, to find nothing, as if lies prevail. Yet many people relied on that falsehood to cast out any allegiance to their officials.

Meanwhile, the story of the Chicago hate attack in the winter of 2019 burst, when the news media ran a false hate story that made headlines and ended up being false when all investigations concluded. The incident took place in Chicago, in 2019, when an actor filed a false claim of being allegedly attacked by two racist men. In America, being racist is a terrible sin, the word itself being the worst insult. A word that stings. When the claim was filed and reported to the news media, a group of activists came out in droves to chant for the actor in support. The media ran the news as if the claim were legitimate and worthy of reporting with conviction of racism and homophobia, instead, it was a lie. Though the essence of journalism is to provide citizens with reliable information through verification and professionalism, the essence of journalism is to report the news as it is, not to give an opinion, and without filter or manipulation. The essence of journalism is to tell the truth. When a lie replaces or overshadows the truth, the consequences can be devastating. Law enforcement investigation later showed the whole story as being a hoax, and the actor was sentenced in 2022. From 2019 to 2022, many Chicagoans were scared of racism in their back yard. How many of them asked if it was true? But the media was on, reminding them of just that, every day. Because society has become one of a single story. Of course, anyone can run with a single story, but the other side of the story is always necessary to complete the story. Anyone can run with a lie, but the truth always catches up. Without seeking to comb through the political propaganda that plays in the web of lies, it is possible to seek to raise awareness of the poisonous impact of lies while cultivating the value of truth.

Sometimes, our refusal to acknowledge that we are being lied to or that something is wrong is our brain's way of coping with the truth. Very often, when people have become accustomed to lies for a very long period of time, they may be reluctant to hear what is true, or a different version of what they know. The change of thoughts may even cause emotional disruption, or create a conflict, and at worst effect a state of denial. It is the current state of society; we reassure ourselves that everything is fine, even when things are not, even when things are false. That reassurance drives people further away from reality, further away from the truth. Nevertheless, the denial convinces people that a lie is not a problem, that the lie only exists in an attempt to correct what they know. A harsh reality that makes society very comfortable in a culture of lies.

What lacks the most in society is the fact that no one questions anything. It is a terrible thing to knowingly tell a lie or make false accusations. And it is much advised not to consider a single story or at least make any accusations and judgments out of it.

'What about the other side of the story?' should be the second question to ask, after, 'is it true?' It may be helpful; it may be the balance needed for a meaningful conversation about the truth. What about holding onto our judgment and checking the other side of the story? For sure, society will be in a much better place.

Single stories have destroyed many people and many things because rushing to judgment with a single story is what characterizes today's society, and unfortunately, at every level. Many have seen representatives be removed from their seats because of allegations, not judgment, but simple allegations that generate mountains of pressure before any investigation is initiated or judgment is made. One representative from the State of New York was recently removed from the congressional seat because of allegations of misconduct, followed by a mountain of pressure. Although the allegation could later be proven as truth, the pressure was founded on one side of the story. Also, the pressure from a single story can be strong when the #MeToo activists move, but people can be resilient if they research the other side of the story. I have witnessed a friend lose his job then his livelihood because of a false accusation of sexual harassment. Losing a job for sexual harassment without judgment spells out condemnation before judgment. Unfortunately, before he was proven innocent of any wrongdoings, the damage had already been done. A loss of a job that caused a loss of livelihood. The consequences of a single story. People become guilty until proven innocent instead, because no one questions what they hear, and it becomes a caveat for destruction with lies. Let us not travel to other parts of the world, where we find similar and even terrible examples of finding a person guilty by a single story. It reminds me of an elementary school teacher and my friend's mother, a woman who struggled because her friends made up a story and told her husband. In a world where nothing was written, and prior to electronic media, it was difficult to prove anything. It was alleged that the friends wanted to destroy her marriage, and they did, because the husband believed in a single story, and sought separation, and remarried. For years, my teacher lived a nightmare, until her prayers worked, her wishes became a command, and she returned with her husband. In between, her livelihood was destroyed, children became disoriented, husband remarried, and problems multiplied. What a single story and a lie can do, in the world where people become guilty until proven innocent instead, and crises multiply.

Vulnerability plays a role as it allows the truth, the lies, and the consequences to manifest. Vulnerability puts a lot of people in a position of lack and want and makes them want to hear specific things that may uplift or make them feel good, and liars prey on those things. Liars tell them exactly what they want to hear, and vulnerable people believe them. When the truth eventually emerges, the vulnerable feel betrayed and lose faith in their ability to make wise judgments. Lying becomes very ordinary, driving society to accept and integrate the behavior. But it should not be, unfortunately. Taking advantage of the vulnerable is already a muddle of its own; it drives the victim to insanity, when the victim has to figure out the truth, find a balance in the midst of seeking truth, and care for their sanity.

It would be a best seller if there were any formula for self-protection against lies. Such protection requires stopping people from telling lies, which is an almost impossible thing to do. It requires accepting society as it is, with its lying track, while seeking to improve what can be improved. In some circumstances, accepting lies may not be a sign of weakness or immorality. Sometimes, it is a sign of strength and wisdom when it is difficult and impossible to overturn a lie. It takes time and some work to get to the truth when a lie has already cast a shadow, and it can be hurtful.

Sometimes, facing the lies first and then dealing with the consequences later is difficult. But the response is far away from anger, and pointing out reality as you see it does not often move anyone out of their state of denial. Acknowledging that people have different perspectives while being clear and not judging anyone is essential. Clearly, discussing different perspectives helps keep a healthy conversation, in the process of healing the rips and tears of lies.

In such a time as this, in a contemporary society where lies have taken root, it is frustrating to witness the belief of the untrue, even when a false story has been proven to be a lie, and at a time when a search for information is at the tip of the fingers. It may be easier to accept that a message is valid than to reject the information it contains, which requires much more cognitive effort to verify its veracity. In other words, believing a lie is much easier than changing your mind about some information already engraved in it. It is even confusing to change your mind and decide what to believe because the new information may also be false.

However, in the end, the question becomes whether the information is useful or not, and if it is, the next question should be whether it is true. Misinformation has taken over; in every area, the sin of the century; whether we are talking about politics, listening to the news media, using social media, or anything affecting the world, the different worldviews that inform our understanding also challenge it at the same time.

It might not be pleasant to engage in a religious and political conversation in an effort to share or influence a different worldview. Also, it is much harder to convince the person's mind and have them understand a fact that differs from their worldview, whether the opinion is based on false information or not. Thus, it should not be a challenge either or a difficult task when presenting the truth, but it is in some cases. Fact and evidence should make a case for the truth, but modern society has twisted every single aspect of everything. Modern culture has changed many definitions and meanings, introducing a lie to change the truth, and therefore, creating confusion that makes the meeting of the minds extremely unattainable. And the trend becomes, let us agree to disagree, even in a simple notion as defining what is a woman.

Unfortunately, because misinformation and disinformation have gained much strength, it is extremely difficult to dislodge or undo a strong belief even if it is erroneous. The persistence of misinformation has some alarming implications when people have based their decisions on that information; at a certain level, to find that the information is false can mean difficulty in reversing one's stance, although it should be relieving.

Though correcting misinformation is a difficult task to take on, it is essential to:

- Focus on the facts, not the myths.
- Fill in the gap of false information where needed.
- Do due diligence and correct the record.
- Keep it simple and avoid misjudgment.
- Consider others' world view and find a middle ground.
- Consider your interlocutor, your audience, and their beliefs.
- Then repeat.

Many individual or social decisions depend on the knowledge and information we receive. Whether accurate or inaccurate, our psychological predispositions and biases make us vulnerable to falsehoods. Because people have a tendency to respond one way compared to another when making some choices, the choice is often based on the information and tools available. Such a way is whatever is favorable to their expectation. Preparing the mind to recognize misinformation that may influence our views is only one step. To battle misinformation, debunking falsehood is also another step. Most importantly, due diligence should not be overrated, as it opens up the possibility of recognizing misinformation then debunking it immediately. Like seeking a doctor when we look to protect our immune system from a virus or foreign invader, our due diligence allows us to discover the truth and strengthen our psychological minds against misinformation that may affect our lives in many ways.

In the search for truth and the rejection of lies, we become passionate about truth. When we pay little attention to the details surrounding us, we may miss the accuracy we are seeking. Imagine scrolling through social media feeds, passing on information, and realizing later that the information is false; then, false information becomes the story circulating from one feed to another. If passing on the information is a form of signing on to its accuracy, refraining from doing so becomes a rejection of lies. And finding the truth requires rejecting the story until its accuracy is established. Media feeds may be something to be careful of, as they hold a lot of untruths in reality.

The search for the truth about everything should not be viewed as a harsh requirement for various reasons. The passion to find the truth about the things that ignite people and the things to learn about for their own sake should be our preoccupation in a present deceitful society. Truth is sought not for status, power, influence, or wealth but because it has intrinsic worth for wellness and a peaceful society. Cultivating an interior life resistant to lies and embracing truth may help to find worthwhile balance, because most of the daily troubles and problems find their sources in a series of lies. Then, embracing the familiar setting of daily life and choosing how to invest in the broader struggle for truth, makes a personal life worthy and meaningful.

6

THE POWER OF WORDS AND LIES

"Words can be deceiving because sometimes when we lie to others, it is because we are also lying to ourselves. That is where the truth is."

– Lori Deschene

Words are not just an utterance of sounds. It is a unit of language that is made up of one or more sounds or written letters that conveys meaning. Words have real power and do more than convey the uttered sounds. Words are spoken when there is something to be said. Words convey information with a tangible impact on people and lives. Words manifest strongly in spirit, with traumatic effects in physical and real life. Undeniably, words are a powerful and unique gift from the creator. Words have the power to make, break, destroy, and build up. Being aware of such power is an opportunity to use words carefully and wisely. Ultimately, every word has an effect and manifests one way or the other; choose words wisely. A lie most often manifests in a word, by a word, and words have power, whether it is the power to build or the power to tear apart. I refer to the power of the tongue that determines life and death biblically.

What does the book of Genesis tell us about the word? That the word is filled with creative power and that words declare things into existence. Because lies are also uttered in words, they ultimately declare things into existence. This tells us what effect lies can have when uttered carelessly. For a peaceful environment, Mark Biddle reminded us in his *Missing the Mark* that lies are a composition of words that should not be used, for such composition of words is put together with no good intention. Words are tools that can bring peace and comfort and make lives better, but like any word, lies can take the opposite end to bring just destruction, chaos, and division, even a health crisis, only to cite these few examples.

Words may not change reality but can change how reality is perceived, thus lies change the perception of reality. Words create filters through which the world is viewed, and a word can mean the difference between liking and disliking the same thing or person. Suppose that someone describes a person that you have never met, or you are about to meet for the first time, as a bad person or as untrustworthy. This builds a predisposition to view that person as untrustworthy regardless of the person's actual level of trustworthiness. Whether you believe the person to be untrustworthy or not, you are already in a different mental state in your approach.

The single word "untrustworthy" creates a filter or dominant effect that predisposes you to view the person you are about to meet as untrustworthy. Thereafter, everything that person says or does may seem untrustworthy and, therefore, creates a sentiment of carefulness, doubt, and even distance and rejection. Although it is good to do so to begin with, it should not be prompted by unnecessary lies but by personal judgment after personal observation that may not end in feelings of untrustworthiness.

Such negative dominant thoughts may be difficult to overcome but it's possible. The more times you meet that "untrustworthy" person and do not experience instances of untrustworthiness, the more likely you are to view the "untrustworthy" person as trustworthy, thus overriding the negative thoughts. However, you are less likely to meet an untrustworthy person the second time because you perceived that person as untrustworthy the first time then had a second thought. This reduces the probability of overcoming negative thoughts that the word itself brought, and that word was a lie.

Thus, the exercise that comes with negative thoughts adds to the negative impact of a lie and the power it has in our lives. Many people live all or the majority of their lives with the wrong perception of other peers because someone who does not like those peers makes a move to convince them using words that can have a negative effect on their person or personality and made that person be viewed differently. And those words created a different and wrong perception of them and annihilated any possibility of collaboration because the power of the lie settled in.

Conversely, if before meeting a person for the first time, a friend tells you that the person you are about to meet is friendly, then you will likely view that person as friendly, regardless of the person's degree of friendliness or non-friendliness. You will tend to excuse the unfriendly behavior if you meet the "friendly" person several times and do not experience friendliness. Such excuses might include any reasons you may find to unsee what you see or to undermine any unfriendly behavior. You will go out of your way to give that person any benefit of the doubt.

Nevertheless, an unfriendly person initially described as friendly gains an advantage from those positive thoughts because people tend to allow the unfriendly person multiple opportunities to demonstrate friendliness despite numerous displays of unfriendly behavior. Meanwhile, opposite reactions often happen when the friendliest ones do not stand a chance, and judgment comes very fast. That affects how information is transmitted and received. In today's busy world, people typically do not consult multiple sources of information to get a balanced view of world events; therefore, the perception of world events comes through the filter created by the first platform or first source.

Social media may currently be the trend, at a time when newspapers are disappearing as a news source, while television newscasts and radio reports become more like propaganda as we know it, despite being the go-to sources of information. However, true information is found in research and analysis, and it may be wise to search multiple sources from different ideologies, then analyze them to find the truth, which most people do not do, but are rather quick to run with the propaganda and lies that are served most often.

These mediums have the power to influence how we view the world with the words they utter as a newscast, and that includes lies, as it has become the trend. Whether those words are news, truth, propaganda, or lies, their programming goals can be effective. Let us talk about a reputable newscast or network introducing a 'bias' to a news story; many people automatically tend to understand a news story as the truth based on that biased filter established by the news media. It may be recommended to pay more attention to what is labeled as the news, then do independent research to reach a new conclusion. The conclusion might be, a high percentage of the time, different from what is called the news. This experience can be educational, setting a new perception of the "news," though the news can set the trend because it has that power.

If, for example, you are listening to what the media calls "a peaceful protest," you may want to step back and search carefully to see if it is peaceful or violent, then determine if the protest is, in fact, peaceful or not. Either you may want to step back and review the definition of the word "peaceful" and determine if the event is peaceful, or if the news is misleading with their own meaning of peaceful. Usually this happens when the news intends to propagate or to promote, and examples are countless. More often, when people are exposed to other more balanced news stories, the prospect of considering others' views becomes a challenge itself, and confusing. Then a battle of views follows, often because most people have listened to one source of information for a long time, to the point it has influenced their ideology and how they think or view the world, whether it is with the truth or lies. At that point, it would be a battle to confront such ideology with another or from a different source of information, looking more like a war between the truth and the lies, because the word has settled in.

One journalist friend explained a scenario of investigation for news stories. The investigation began with interviewing a suspect who was thought to have kidnapped a four-year-old little girl. However, before talking to the suspect, the investigator had already made a decision about this person because the allegations against him were convincing. As a result, everything the suspect said to the investigator during the interview was viewed as an indication of guilt. The more questions she asked of him, the more anxious he became, not because he was guilty and facing years in prison for something he did not do, but because she thought he was guilty, no matter what he said. Needless to say, my journalist friend learned a hard lesson from this experience and was somehow embarrassed when the real kidnapper was identified. These negative thoughts are the root of much false information and a combination of words and lies that create confusion in people.

As the title of this section suggests, this gives you an example of how words are powerful, especially when we look at the word 'interrogation,' which is quite different from the word 'interview.' Interrogations are often viewed as adversarial, and whether consciously or unconsciously, the person doing the interrogating often forms a guilty opinion of the person being questioned simply because the person was brought in for questioning. And the interrogation/interview becomes the paradigm that creates two negative filters: confrontational and perceived guilt because the word itself creates such a description.

The interrogation form becomes confrontational when the interviewers go into the interrogation with a preconceived notion that the suspect will be challenging or argumentative. And the slightest provocation by the suspect triggers more aggressive responses, which the interviewer will often anticipate. The same actions that interviewers perceive as aggressive during interrogations would probably be judged as less aggressive or neutral during interviews because interviewers perceive interviews as non-confrontational. It appears that the whole scenario depends on the perception, the perception of which originating from the word interrogation. The word that settled in the mind and created the perception of things, of people, and therefore guides the event.

The second negative filter is that interviewers will likely view the interviewees as guilty before the interrogations commence, perceive everything the interviewees say or do to support their guilt, and discount or excuse away any evidence that does not support their preconceived notion of guilt. An alternative interview/interrogation paradigm approach may be placed on a resistance continuum. At one end of the continuum, interviewees offer information without resistance.

Conversely, interviewees are reluctant to provide information or just fall silent. This concept allows investigators to glide back and forth along the resistance continuum using specialized techniques to overcome varying degrees of resistance. Sounding like a game of words and their power. Interviewers focus on the appropriate ways to overcome witnesses' and suspects' resistance. As the interviewee's resistance increases or decreases, the interviewer adjusts the intensity of the inquiry by selecting suitable words to overcome the interviewee's resistance, developing competing suggestions or thoughts as an educated guess that supposes a different outcome based on the same or similar set of circumstances.

For example, when I speak with someone, I hypothesize that the person is telling the truth. However, a competing hypothesis suggests that the person is lying. Therefore, evidence seeks to support the initial or competing suggestion during a conversation. Therefore, dishonest people say and do things that make them look honest, knowingly telling lies to appear as honest as possible.

The next time you meet a new colleague, interview someone, or buy a new product, think about how you came to form your opinion about that person or product. Chances are high that your opinions were formed by preconceived thoughts or importance from a word. Anyone can enhance or hurt their opportunities depending on their first impressions of what is at stake. That is when reputation is capital as it precedes their arrival. Reputation comes from words and how far they have traveled and what effect they have. These reasons brought Spurgeon to the statement that: "A lie will go round the world while the truth is pulling its boots on," creating a bad reputation along the way because a lie has power as well as a word. We should be careful about subjecting anyone to a lie because it may be killing a person's reputation. Choose words wisely.

The Dominion Power of Word

To put the thought of a word as a gift into perspective, let us start at the very beginning, when God placed Adam and Eve in the Garden of Eden. He made it clear that they and their descendants were to have "dominion" over all the earth, in Moses 2:26; or, in other words, they were to have presiding and governing power on the earth. A word that is treated as a gift without which a purpose cannot be fulfilled. It is the gift of using words to create language, a way of communicating. The first task was to name things and define relationships that established order and dominion. From the same perspective, language can be as destructive as it is creative, because it is a combination of words that can include what is true and what is a lie.

The verbal exercise allowed the record and transmission of information from generation to generation, allowing humans to maintain dominion. The power of words remains the primary means by which men and women try to exercise dominion or influence in the world. The same power plays when we replace words with lies; then, we have the same influence. Influence that is in its finest spiritual manifestation as well as in other areas as the political and the emotional. Let alone be a lie that also influences the same with the damages that it may bring.

From a financial standpoint, let us consider how words affect the world economically. Millions of dollars are spent each year carefully crafting the messages we see and hear in advertising, from the self-indulgent to the cleverest saying. I have always been amused by commercials that say, "Nothing tastes better (or washes better) than brand X." If that is the case, I should buy nothing because it sounds like a lie. Companies recognize the power of words when they name products. If the product has an appealing or special name, it can be sold in high demand for a higher price; hence, designer labels are effective, and commercially, word sells.

Of course, if a name becomes associated with negative connotation, it can also negatively affect the sales of the product. Gerald Erichsen described General Motors' embarrassment in his piece *"The Chevy Nova That Wouldn't Go"* to explain how GM introduced its new Chevy Nova to Latin America and learned that in Spanish, "NO VA" meant "it doesn't go." Later, automobile manufacturers became very cautious in naming cars because any word, lie, or name has power. For a time, they used animal names: Cougar, Lynx, Mustang, Cobra, etc. Then they cautiously settled for two- or three-syllable names that ended with the vowel '*a*' and sounded a little Japanese. They considered Acura, Sentra, and Mazda, to name a few, and the similarities were not coincidental. Likewise, some time ago, pharmaceutical companies found that if the names of their products ended in "-in," they would sell well. Thus, because the goal is to sell, they would lie to make it sell. From an assessment of a pharmaceutical advertisement analysis published by the American Journal of Pharmaceutical Education, they illustrated this, using examples like aspirin, penicillin, Coracidin, Pamprin, and Colistin, to mention just a few.

With the advent of modern information technologies, linguistic messages have flooded the current generation with great influence on the economy. The proliferation of credit cards and loan offers is one of the effects of the word and lies. The business world is very much aware of such power. Thus, words influence every aspect of life, and so do lies.

Politically, what would politics be without the power of words? In other words, the power of lies? In politics, words inform and persuade, words manipulate, words inspire, words speak truth, and words tell half-truths and lies too. With the passage of time through earlier millennia, some sacred uses of language undoubtedly became corrupted and used not only for sacred purposes but also for political purposes. For example, in some preliterate cultures in which no one knew how to read or write, a shaman or other leader maintained political power by relying on incantations and the "power" of secret or special words to accomplish specific tasks. In early Finnish oral traditions in which knowledge was acquired through vocal utterance, one's ability to recite the right words determined social position and power.

In modern society, shamans have been replaced by advertisers, spin doctors, televangelists, and sometimes demagogues. The Nazis' use of language successfully mobilized a nation and gained the allegiance of many to do things they would never do on their own initiative. The language utilized by totalitarian regimes was effective in misinforming and withholding information in an attempt to control people. Many modern nations are guilty of what has been called "doublespeak" in using euphemistic terms and dense jargon to mask unpleasant realities and to control public opinion. Politicians often doublespeak by deliberately distorting the meaning of words to fit what they want to portray, and sometimes, the zeal for a political cause motivates people to misrepresent the truth with shocking words to achieve their ends.

The misrepresentations seem obvious, often ludicrous, when directed at an opponent that they want to label as unqualified and not worthy of attention or consideration. Such misrepresentations are often very blatant when they occur within our own front yard. The fast-paced world today has given rise to a sound-bite culture in which half-truths can be quickly disseminated without adequate discussion or rebuttal to gain a good understanding of a person or an issue; the accurate platform of what plays in modern politics. We hear the word "racist" in every sentence when it comes to politics, and because the word has been played for so long and about everything, it diminishes the true meaning of such an overused word. Politicians use that word to stimulate emotion and provoke people to vote in a certain way.

With power in words, misuse achieves political ends that can cause many problems before they are exposed. In contemporary recorded history, it has contributed to wars, martyrdoms, or character assassinations. Fortunately, speaking the truth with plainness and admiration does not come as a reward but as a standard, the integrity of speaking the truth. However, in this modern world of lies, men and women of integrity hold onto trust and hope for a better tomorrow.

One of the most necessary parts of the use of language is the notion of the "definition." When the definitions of words are agreed upon, the discourse becomes productive. It should not be a simple, convenient definition but a set term that is accurate, complete, and true. When special interests are at stake, definitions become critical lines of defense. Every word is twisted in the direction of interest for the sake of definition. Even the legal world has embraced the trend; in some legal cases, the outcome may depend on the definition of one or a few words. Personal fortunes, careers, and life-and-death decisions can turn on the definition of a single word.

Definitions have been used throughout history to justify horrible things. In wartime, enemies are labeled with terms that make them seem less than human, so killing them is more tolerable because one can rationalize it's not a human being killed. For example, slavery and the atrocities of the Holocaust were perpetuated by defining African Blacks and Jews, respectively, as less than human. In reality, even though the label was a lie, using a different word to characterize a human being, it carried the power of something less than human to commit the atrocities.

History has shown that the definition of words is capital. As definitions change, so do perceptions, and changes in behavior do not lag far behind. Unfortunately, some modern uses of racist language are not far from the same abuses, and everything becomes racist when convenient, depending on how the word "racist" is defined. To avoid the lies that hide in the definition of a word, let us be on guard to keep focus on accuracy, honesty, and truth.

Emotionally, words also affect us. It works through language that even includes lies. Language use and abuse does not only have an economic or political impact, but also carries a very personal and emotional component. The power of words and language is not limited to what or whom it can control. In fact, one of the most significant functions of language is entirely beyond our conscious control. Language may even control us. Language is a function that establishes our identities. Few things are closer to our personal group or national identities than our language. Few things affect us more emotionally than hearing our language. And imagine when that language is filled with what is not true and the power and impact it has on our identity.

Calling someone outside of what he bears as a name may be as hurtful as the use of unkind or unwise words; understanding that words hurt, as do unkind words and lies. As children, we heard, "Sticks and stones may break my bones, but names will never hurt me." It is only a display of courage and strength, but that is false, especially for those who were called by different names growing up, such as stupid, ugly, dumb, or any unkind words other than their names. The truth is, they still remember decades later and may remember for the rest of their lives. Often, some damage done by words can be worse than through physical violence because words matter, so let them not be filled with lies. In reality, words should be used as carefully as we would use our hands because both can have devastating effects and bring long-lasting pain. As dangerous as a hand or fist can be hurting someone physically, words can do the same emotionally and spiritually.

Brigham Young taught an exciting principle in his devotional: by controlling our words, we gain control of our thoughts. By controlling our tongues, we gain control over our minds. We must fortify ourselves against others' language that influences us emotionally, whether vulgar or hurtful, and the lies told against us to negate any influence the falsehood may have on people. If one is confident in his own abilities and can be hurt by falsehood over time, we must recognize the long-lasting power of unkind words, and the long-lasting power of lies.

Spiritually, as we link the power of the word to the economy, politics, and emotions in every area of our lives, the spiritual aspect of words can be incredible because the word is the spirit itself. The spiritual power of words is their ability to penetrate the soul, their ability to inspire, and when they do, let it be good works and have positive effects wherever they are heard. Words also bring peace to hearts and minds through kind expressions and wise counseling. Their spiritual effect begins with hearing, and hearing alone brings the effect that the word carries. Now, let us replace the word here with lies and imagine the opposite. That is exactly what happens with lies.

Words of confession lift the burdens of wrongdoings as much as words of agreement place one under a covenant. That's how powerful a word can be, and from the biblical perspective, God manifests through the word, and when He speaks, it manifests. Because words have power, so do lies. And certainly, they manifest into existence.

Ever notice how great souls behave mildly when they perform spiritual deeds? Because it is true, truth does not need embellishment; straightforward language is powerful, and it rings true in spirit. While language or communication is important in all relations, it is especially so in every aspect of our lives. What is said may become reality just by listening and believing; although it does manifest in the physical, it cannot be seen, but it exists in spirit, and when a lie is told, it manifests and even leaves a stigma. It has been so throughout time, from the beginning with the words in the book of Genesis: "Let there be light," and there was light.

When we understand how our deeply felt emotions are evoked more accurately and meaningfully by words, they help us understand why it is important to select what we listen to, as the significance of the words is receptive to the "workings of the Spirit." Such realization, combined with an awareness of the other influences of words we have previously discussed, should lead us to a reverence for the considerate, careful, truthful, and ethical use of language, for the very words we speak shape our beliefs, define our dominions, and create the emotional, intellectual, and spiritual worlds in which we live. In other words, the lies that are listened to and the falsehoods that are perpetrated shape the beliefs, define the dominions, and create the emotional, intellectual, and spiritual worlds around us.

Inasmuch as words can breed love or hate and even violence, especially when those words become lies, words can also empower and be life-giving, such as words of love and compliment. Consequently, the negative effect of lies and falsehoods ignites crises that can only find a solution in their positive side. And the positive aspect only comes with ensuring that every word we speak is true and accurate. If we believe the words "Let there be light" and there was light, we can also believe that words such as "I don't like this person" may only create hate. Realize that hearing this person is bad only creates that image in your mind, and you begin to see the person as bad, even if the person is not a bad person, but the word itself has already penetrated your subconscious mind.

Look around, listen to politicians, and realize why they always seek to convince the masses that their opponent is the worst human being. They understand the power of the word, whether it is true or not. They want a vote and will say anything to keep voters away from their opponents. Unfortunately, most of the time, they are able to convince the vulnerable, because it works. Lies have power.

7
THE IMPACTS OF LIES

"Anybody can tell lies. There is no merit in a mere lie; it must possess art, it must exhibit a splendid and plausible and convincing probability; that is to say, it must be powerfully calculated to deceive."

– *"My First Lie and How I Got Out of It"* by Mark Twain

It is familiar that lies are a part of our lives and that it is human and usual behavior to lie. When its entrenchment becomes a poison to society, the question reverts to its allowability. Lies are repeated and prevalent because they are allowed. They have the impact that builds up or the impact that tears down a culture. Surely lies have the power to positively or negatively affect our lives. As a person who has lived through the impact of lies, I have experienced the numerous shocks of being lied about, from growing up through my teenage years, then as an adult, as I continue to, I have witnessed adults doing the worst kind of lying. Kids often lie small lies like "I did not break a glass." Teens lie like "don't talk to that person, because she said… he said." Although kids' little lies and teens' frequent lies can be hurtful, adults' lies are worse. They can destroy relationships and livelihoods. And such destruction only happens if no one dares to ask if it is true. Thus, lying may be human, but it should not be considered normal. Lying is deceitful behavior; it is a shameful act; it exposes the liar's false pretense and devalues his personality. It is often treated as a taboo, as it should be.

Let us not be deceived to think that lying is an attribute of youth. Lying has become highly destructive of values, of people, and society as a whole, particularly when encouraged and not challenged or rebuked. Not only is lying a sign of a significant concern or a bigger problem with the person telling something that is not true, but the person may also expect his action to be a solution to the problem. It is also a bigger problem when the person telling the lies can get away with it.

However, when situations are mixed with lies, trust may vanish and completely flip the scope of a relationship that is built on it. Imagine the circumstances of a divorce, in which the evildoers seek to flip the story to portray themselves as the righteous ones while making every effort possible to shift the blame for any wrongdoings to the other party. When it is open season of finger-pointing, the fireworks of lies become very effective. Because society has normalized and encouraged lies as if every story is true, no questions are asked.

I found myself in a scheme that involved an ex-relationship, in front of what is called a traditional court in a village in Africa, where I was born. The Kingship plays a traditional administration of justice. Whenever there is a problem, a time-honored tribunal may hear the parties in the kingdom. I learned this the hard way when I found myself in that sort of traditional setting after a formal legal proceeding that certainly was not pleasant. Accused with a fabricated story that suggested I had an ex-partner expelled from the country, I was mortified. At a time in society when lies have replaced a weapon and become one, I was discomfited by being looked at as this unrighteous person who committed such an egregious act, and one for sure I did not do. Walking down to be heard, the perception was that I was a horrible and wicked person to be afraid of, only because they had heard and never questioned what they'd heard and never asked themselves, is it true? The experience was heavy and unpleasant, until my side of the story was heard, then I was relieved. And after the hearing, I felt what difference the question, is it true? can make. The answer to that question brings clarity, it brings the other side of the story, and the solution to what can be solved.

Remember, liars always find something hurtful to use against others, something their victims despise the most and then accuse them of doing it. It can be something that liars do, but they project it onto others, and in the worst way possible. The truth was that the supposedly expelled person carefully made a thoughtful and personal decision to leave the country, and maybe things did not go the way he wanted. The next thing I knew, I found myself sitting in front of the King, having to defend myself against such accusations, having to brave the "Where is she?"; "How can she do such things?"; "I cannot believe she could do that"; and, "How wicked is that?" What went through my mind at the time was the stoning in the Bible. But staying truthful and confident was my strength, that is what I know for sure.

This is a culture in which lies are prevalent, and others' opinions matter; then, when opinions get mixed with lies, they matter even more. Honestly, I was grateful the King took the steps to listen to my side of the story. He did not only believe what he heard, but he questioned the nature of the story, then asked what happened and listened to the full story, the history, and the details of it, to understand the full scope of the matter. I appreciated His Majesty's "Is it true?" moment more than words can translate, because considering one side of the story only is itself damaging; unfortunately, a single story prevails in a culture of lies.

In such a culture, very few can do the same. A simple "your fiancé is my ex-girlfriend," whether it is true or not, but very often false, can result in the engagement being over, the marriage canceled, and a proper investigation to diminish doubt does not take place. Many can testify to this scheme, because a lie is a weapon; want to kill something? Just spread a lie on top, then it is over. Because the spread is wild, and the victim keeps the scars. If only society understood the impact of a single story, the negative effect of judging without checking, and taking the necessary steps to do so, it would be a much better and more peaceful place; it would heal society.

The whole experience was very hurtful, but it was a lesson-learning experience. I grew tired of explaining myself and the situation to those who tried to listen. Many did not. Instead, they ran with one side of the story and painted a different picture of who I am and took pleasure in doing it. I am sure many people have been in a situation of being charged with a lie or stigmatized for what they had nothing to do with. But it's irrelevant to look past the concern to overcome the pain that comes with the experience. No one has the responsibility to force honesty onto others; it is our collective effort to check the veracity of information we receive and the other side of a story. If we do not, we will have no standing to make any judgment or decision.

No one can control others' actions, but anyone can control the effect of any scheme and undermine the goal. The reality is simple: every word has an effect, whether positive or negative, whether accurate or a lie. Liars rely on the power that a word carries, to manipulate and reach his goal, which is difficult to reverse because it may be too late. Reversing a lie is like ironing a wrinkled paper to read what is written on it and expecting not to find the lines. Undermining the goal of lying will mean standing against the negative scheme that may be at play.

What we do and what happens in our lives shapes who we are. We can reverse lies and tell a different and truthful story, an accurate story about ourselves, with our own words and actions. The stories we tell about our experiences and our interpretations shape us even more. Sometimes, hearing and believing we are not the subject of stories put out in the world is hard because it is a story told by others. And to know our image out in the world is not an accurate depiction of ourselves is even harder because the inaccurate depiction by others is well-intentioned.

When we are targeted specifically, the stories told may not reflect our true experience or portray our true value or who we are and who we know ourselves to be; but what is out in public is a different story of us, tinted with lies. Imagine reconnecting with an old circle, after years or decades of being portrayed as someone you are not, for having done nothing wrong, and do not aspire to do, and will possibly never do, then when all the facts are gathered together to show your innocence, you understand the vice that has decayed society.

The consequences of such decay are countless. The breakdowns in relationships, in families, the mistrust in different groups and networks become prevalent, with negative effects on society as a whole. Relationships suffer and the children involved deal with the fallout. While adults can easily handle troubled relationships, the trouble is often harder on the children and younger generation who can no longer play or party with their friends because the parents in troubled relationships cannot meet any longer. Because a single-story stance is a travesty, opportunities for networking and partnerships are often missed as consequences, and the list goes on. The reality is that everyone misses out, people always fall into such a snare, and no one reaps any benefit.

Thinking about it for a moment; it is a forceful process for being part of society; no one makes that choice but can only make a choice on how to live and belong to that society. It is prevalent that society forces the course with lies as they gain strength increasingly. While lying may count as human nature, the contrary can also be true, and the truth is that human nature is love and care; human nature is not destructive; that's why punishment exists, in order to punish wrongdoings like lies. Considering lying as human nature is like giving everyone a pass to lie or rewarding it, and lying becomes a cancer to society, which demands a cure for a peaceful society. The cure begins with doubt, skepticism, and questioning what we hear. The cure follows by not making a decision or judgment based on what we hear without checking the authenticity of it. The cure continues with rejecting false information and making sure it is true.

Society can be easily fixed or destroyed depending on the information that influences it. Let us say you form a view of a celebrity from the information you receive from the media, without knowing anything else about them; then you will realize that the media and other news feed us what they want us to believe about that particular person. There may be lots of projection, blame, and judgment as if that celebrity directly affects our lives somehow, even though they often do to a certain degree. Some are highly influential and followed, because people believe in what is projected of them and how they want to be seen; projection which is often effected with lies and simple actions. Even though the world of celebrities may be far from reality, their seldom appearances often show that most have nothing to add to ordinary people's domain or realm of life, except inspiration; yet they are followed and influential in the wrong way instead. Public figures like Jada Pinkett Smith and Will Smith were once portrayed as a perfect couple and admired all over the world. Until the day they aired their own public conversation, then published a book, then the truth came out that it was not as perfect as portrayed. Thus, the first information of a perfect couple sent out a false impression. Thus, there are lots of lies behind the screens that boost followers' dreams, and the couple exposed such lies. Sometimes whatever they say is taken as a word of wisdom, but it should not always be just because of celebrity status but because it must be truly wise. In fact, it is essential to focus on what is real and true, not on power and flow, because perversion may come through the media, using celebrities.

One way to distinguish reality from false information is how information affects our perception of things; it is in the interactions with the people around and who are part of the stories themselves. It can be difficult to distinguish between a perception of a person's journey and a projection that comes with the information received, and lies often play a role in between.

Projection is one mechanism to place one's own label on another person, and a lie often perfectly plays that role. More likely, the story someone else wants to tell about others carries great influence, making ground for external validation because influence comes with insecurity, insecurity that invites the lies forth, and the projection of self-pain to others. The whole mechanism opens a caveat for lies or truth, to interfere with and guide the perception of what is being portrayed. And lies often prevail. This happens for people-pleasers with a strong desire to meet the expectations of who others want them to be. Remember you can't please everyone, yet when you try to please someone, you will please everyone, and no one will be satisfied until focus is placed on the truth and logic. Sometimes, people get magnified as superhuman, making themselves feel suitable for the moment while it is fleeting, and most of the time it is fleeting because it is a lie.

Unfortunately, disappointment follows the belief in external validation that is expected from others. The same can be said about believing anything we see or hear because it is said with a charming attitude that makes anyone believe without question. Tellers of lies can sometimes be charismatic, with the characteristics associated with friendliness and honesty. However, charm and charisma are used as cover-ups for lies, so others do not see the real person behind the mask; liars never want to be suspected of who they are and will do anything to cover up.

When confronting reality, it can be fascinating to witness a disagreement between two people with different views, each claiming their view to be closer to reality or their story to be correct and that everyone else should align and do something about it. No, a point of view should be a personal take; whether it is accurate or not, it should not be forced onto others. This happens in politics. The question becomes, what is the disagreement about? Is it someone else's need for us to be similar, different, or fit into others' box? Or is it to agree to someone else's wants? What if it is a lie? The main question returns: is it true? The question that should guide every conversation or understanding. Nevertheless, walking on a path of integrity, a personal path of change and growth without following others' views, requires keeping a line of logic and truth.

Notwithstanding, people always have a choice until differences settle. One person's expectations of another can change or shift, often without a sign or warning. And the other side of the coin does not always change in value, but the other side of a story can change the story. When it does, the other side becomes either a tool for confirmation of the story or a tool to distort the truth. Nevertheless, the focus must remain on what is true.

Sometimes lies can also get mixed into the other side of a story and may confuse the situation. The downfall happens when people cave in or upend their lives because of it, and they believe the story they carry in their mind about others, because of what was told with a twist of lies. They keep their own portrait of others according to that belief and to what they were told. Unfortunately, the whole process outlines a circle of lies. The culture is that people listen and believe or choose to believe whatever they are told; they might not have a very good understanding of the scheme and might have constant concern with what to believe. But it is always good to know the truth. The motivation factor may be considered, as well as the reasons behind the story, whether to correct or to confirm the record. Many see life as a race to the top, and some will do whatever it takes to get there, including trying to undermine others with lies injected in while talking about them. Interestingly a negative conversation about something, or someone who is disliked, is assumed to be true, no question asked, because the wish is to hear more, and more leads to seeing a person in a different light.

First, it is good to know what to believe and to have the power to hold onto that belief. Lies often come in many ways, in the form of complaint, or simply distorting the truth for one reason or another. As the saying goes for those who complain the most, it is easier to look at others and assign blame to them for any wrongs or failures, than it is to understand how to step up and face a bull, instead of complaining through lies to the self and to others. For any business not growing, abundance not flowing, relationships not working, and for not being happy, easy is to assign blame by telling stories that have nothing to do with reality. Yet, telling stories that have nothing to do with reality is somewhat a lie, to shift blames to others instead of taking accountability. Even though the blame comes from the belief that it is true, one realizes what to do about it. Examples are countless around communities, and alone, can fill these pages. As long as the truth is told in a story, the value of truth should not be questioned. Whether the reality is apparent or not, it still affects the health of society.

Believing in oneself and in truth is a strong sense of self that no lie can take away. And lies should not be a permission for, or a denial of, who we are. There may be a choice to make, a choice to stand strong against lies or melt into the depression that lies bring, a choice to be guided by the truth, and not let any lie trouble our journey. With a mindset free of lies, everything depends on us, not the tellers of lies. In the meantime, it is our duty to do our due diligence to make sure we do not facilitate the implementation of lies in culture; a peaceful society depends on it.

Though feelings are never completely wrong, the beliefs that cause those feelings often are. When emotions like anger, frustration, sadness, disappointment, happiness, or pride settle within, the wrongs, the lies, or the ugly are often the cause. Feeling our own feelings is essential; we may not even know why and especially how, but we very often fall on the "not liking" side. And we do whatever we can to avoid some feelings. Those feelings often drive us in the right or wrong direction, and unfortunately, lies can be the driving force. They connect us to ourselves and to others, and while not always pleasant, it is easy to understand why the feelings and the messages we communicate are essential. And the messages should be communicated accurately, because if lies get in the way, the emotional message sent could be wrong as well.

Instead, if we close off our emotions or get disconnected from our own and others' beliefs, it leads us to uncertainty. It may even direct us to making bad choices. Suppressing our emotions and beliefs because we are subject to others' lies about us may be harmful to our well-being. Suppressing emotions and beliefs may not be a cure, but controlling and adjusting the feelings accordingly may be. For many, the disconnect happens when people get caught up in their own feelings. No matter how strong anyone may be, it always occurs at some point either to be upset or to be affected by lies, which prompts the feeling of sadness. These emotions are impacted by beliefs about feelings, which are tied to culture, and have a significant impact as well. The reality is, if feelings take the driver's seat, or if lies take the driver's seat, any vehicle may take the wrong direction, and this also applies to our lives.

Of course, culture plays a big role in shaping character, like today, in the 21st century particularly, the time of upside down, when lies equate truth shamelessly, what was once innocent until proven guilty becomes guilty until proven innocent. Emotions have become the determining factor of anything, including what is true and what is false, while lies motivate such emotions.

Our beliefs play an important role in how we do or don't express or process our feelings about situations. Ultimately, feelings lead us in any direction and may bring us further from the goal or purpose of the emotion in the first place. And those feelings and emotions also help concoct stories, mostly false ones. For example, saying, "My colleague does not like me," or "My in-law doesn't like me," is not an emotion but an extension of the actions that trigger those emotions, whether the statement is true or not. However, if the statement becomes, "I feel angry," that is a clear statement, an extension of emotion, and all sorts of emotions will surround that anger, from being frightened, anxious, or troubled. We disguise our thoughts as feelings to shield ourselves, and surely staying authentic and truthful only might save us from such trouble. It is quite common to disguise some thoughts as feelings to self-protect or shield from actual feelings, the internal feelings that often lead to the path of falsehood.

The stories we hear often sound like limiting beliefs; some of those stories may be true, but many are not. Being in a position to hurl some untrue stories may raise some questions. Getting over what is often designated as upbringing may be a helpful trial to understanding and solving complex situations. It may also be helpful to interpret and understand the depth of the underlying stories. Support is necessary, but despite the strong support that some have, it may still not be enough when one's mental state does not bring the person to understand its importance, and then complaining and worrying about the lack of support becomes second nature. Understanding such a mix of feelings, emotions, and their origins will help to quickly shed some effects of lies and false stories. Lies create confusion that only the truth can solve, and lying often comes from within to justify some behaviors. Thus, lies impact lives in many ways.

The remedies reside in setting emotional boundaries, maintaining healthy and reciprocal relationships, building and nurturing trust, and acting essentially on self-respect and self-protection that provide the strength and clarity to take the right direction. A direction of authenticity and truth. Relationships energize and make others feel important, acknowledged, welcomed, embraced, and encouraged under the effects of lies, in the interest of self-care. How effective this communication and embrace could be to help cure the cancer that society has nurtured with the culture of lies. And that's how society can heal from lies, heading towards a healthy and peaceful culture.

8

HOW LYING AFFECTS CHARACTER

"When lying and omission become part of your character, you lose integrity and the trust you once had from others."

– Theodore Walter Fedorchak

One of the *Ten Commandments* addressed what society was or could become in terms of a human being's nature to lie and how far lying can go, and for that reason, it prescribed that one shall not bear false witness against his neighbor; this means that one shall not intentionally make a false statement, or in other words, one shall not lie. T.W. Fedorchak made it very simple. He stated: "When lying and omission become part of your character, you lose integrity and the trust you once had from others." Additionally, when you do, you destroy your personality, and you destroy others' personality and character in the process. Thus, the world could be a much better and peaceful place without a lie, yet based on many years of experience and inquiry, there are all sorts of verbal and non-verbal prompts that clearly and completely give away the truth.

The loss of integrity and the broken trust with others begin with the closest of relationships including relatives, friends, acquaintances, and even colleagues. What does that say about a person who tells a lie, and how does that affect one's character? What does that say about society? Ultimately, lies affect society at many levels, and an epidemic of lies could translate to a society that tolerates and facilitates falsehood. An epidemic of lies would manifest in deliberation and freedom to lie without regard, remorse, or consequences. Whether a lie may cause ruin or not, it is up to what is, and to the ones affected to seek any reparation for the negative consequences.

While freedom of speech allows a person to speak freely, it is arguable that freedom of speech includes freedom to lie. As long as the speech does not cause harm to a person or his reputation, whether a financial loss, emotional stress, or even mental deprivation, the person is free to express his opinion without fear, whose opinion may spell lies depending on how it is stated. When such freedom becomes a gateway to lying, it may be interesting to filter the lies to avoid any defamation that may ruin one's reputation.

Defamation damages reputation and often comes as a consequence of knowingly divulging information that is not true about others. And the phenomenon negatively infects society to such a degree that truth becomes a derision. If only freedom to express opinion meant freedom to tell the truth, many would certainly seek to redefine truth. In such a society as this, defamation becomes a daily activity for those who find it professes to attack anyone's character with lies against the person.

Although these actions are punishable by law, society has undermined the disorderly and punishable aspects of the actions by normalizing falsehood and lies. By doing so, the harm to reputation resulting from those who lie, defame, bully, harass, shame, or stalk becomes normal. And by normalizing lies, untrue allegations, and unethical and dishonest behavior, these actions often go unpunished. Unfortunately, such behavior has become a cultural thing. One may think that the court is there to solve problems of all sorts, but it is often disappointing that the court can only do so much, given the frequency and high cost of the legal processes. Thus, victims of lies and defamation, particularly, are often unable to pursue or prove such allegations, and continue to suffer the pains that may be internal but often succeed in destroying the character's or reputation.

What does lying say about one's character? Until the culture truly characterizes a lie as wrongdoing that is bad for society, many continuously get away with it and even believe that lying is another way of life. This creates different problems for everyone in a circle: the teller of lies, the truth-teller, the listeners, the victims, and everyone around. Growing up, I was taught, like many, lessons about honesty, good manners, respect, courtesy, civility, politeness, and always telling the truth. Being honest and telling the truth is part of a strong, good, and peaceful character that allows people to feel good about themselves, make others feel good, and keep the peace. As we have learned from the *Ten Commandments*, the rule is, and shall always be, thou shall not lie.

Unfortunately, the battle between the truth and lies was already going, and that commandment was written as prevention. When a motivation to lie takes precedence over honesty, lying becomes a loose-leaf behavior, playing in every direction when convenient. Usually, the desire for compassion plays a role, as most people may tell lies to seek compassion, favor, advantage, or dominion. The bearers of false witness do not often care about hurting others or causing any pain in general; they care more about themselves and how to make the lies beneficial. Even though it means misrepresenting how they feel about themselves and even the receiver, it may also be about a person or someone near and dear to them, but it often does not matter.

What a liar cares the most about is compassion, manipulation, and anything that is to his benefit. Character and reputation become meaningless. With the conviction that his interlocutors will not question what they hear and because the heart of a human is meant to love, help, give, and protect, then lies become an easy shot to manipulate into believing without question. Eventually, they realize they have been lied to, and what may have happened in the meantime contributes to a fallen society. A society that has fallen away from the standards that define a moral society.

According to Levine and Schweitzer (2013, 2015), those who tell prosocial lies are often viewed as more trustworthy and moral than those who tell harsh truths. While lies seem to be seductive, truth only seeks righteousness. Moreover, prosocial lies seek to form more extensive social networks that can be manageable. This makes lying driven by the sentiment of compassion yield many benefits.

In contrast, lies not motivated by compassion constrain the size of social networks and, therefore, may yield fewer benefits. Lies may have become the rule and the truth the exception. When indolence and the failure to conduct research to determine the truthfulness have facilitated the process, it may lead society to a place where we believe the lie more quickly than we believe the truth. And by the time we come to the truth, the damage of the lies has already been done, a translation of how lies travel faster than the truth. Whoever has never found himself in such a scenario may only have to look closely around.

This reminds me of my being removed from a network I was part of, with no questions asked, because it was alleged that I'd contributed to suing the network for some reason. Completely cut off any communication, invite or salutation, guilt by association grew; thus, my confidence and honesty strengthened me in the process. Years later when every scheme fell apart, I was reconsidered, no need for justification.

This also reminds me of this marvelous friend, an educator, who left the school one day in handcuffs and lost his job immediately after being accused of sexual harassment and improper touching. It appears that every definition has evolved in recent years, including physical education and instruction guidelines, which may be under revision with more boundaries to be set. While the presumption of innocence requires that one be presumed innocent until proven guilty, the new trend will presume you are guilty until you are proven innocent. By the time you are proven innocent, you will have already served a sentence because people believe everything they are told is true and condemn without evidence.

For only being falsely accused by a student who even described physical education as punishment, my friend lost his job before he had a chance to respond in court to prove his innocence. And the damage amidst the process was quite unbearable. That is society in the 21st century. If only we could very often ask, "Is it true?" we could march toward a more collaborative and peaceful society.

Lying is often motivated by the desire for material gains, with the negative consequences it may cause, not only for the person trying to deceive others but also for those deceived by lies. Telling lies out of self-interest makes deceptive behavior become a social norm. Lying is sometimes socially contagious; if precedent shows that dishonesty is appropriate, rewarded, or unpunished, people will tend to be more likely to lie. That simply is human behavior. Gino, Francesca, who studied human behavior in communities, shows "the effect of one bad apple on the barrel," and although people emulate the dishonesty of those they consider to be in their "in-group," they become less likely to lie when they observe out-group members being dishonest.

When lying becomes a social currency embraced by those who benefit the most from it, the question of moral character becomes the decisive factor that can help prevent people from lying for personal gain. Everybody wants to view themselves as good people, and they find a way to justify their dishonesty. They justify their lies with other lies, and so on. The small initial lies escalate into other forms of dishonesty, making it more difficult to notice a slow erosion of integrity, moral code, beliefs, values, and principles, and therefore, attacks a person's character through that process, undermining the rules of integrity; as if lying has no boundaries.

Rules are forgotten as the person doing the lying presents themselves as virtuous while condemning others for the same type of lies or deception that they themselves created. Many may even be often compensated for past lies through justifications for their behavior while trying not to realize or expose their wrongdoings, their lies, or their prosocial actions that have destroyed others. With every effort to cover their lies with lies, they put themselves in a positive light, and when they feel they have gotten away with deceptive behavior, it takes them out of a mindset that requires them to follow any rule. Now, they believe they can get away with anything. As a result, creative justice flows; it allows the person telling lies about other lies to produce new ideas, good or bad, or even new lies.

Deception comes at a price when driven by desire, and some liars forget that their dishonesty may have contributed to their success or their failure. Lying may have taken them to where they are. In reality, the consequences can spell a more complex ending. It may be correct that lies breed contempt and guilt, or maybe they do much more. Lies foster relationships; lies create and destroy social networks, and ruin people's character and reputation in the process.

Understanding why people lie goes a long way in predicting which consequences may result from dishonesty. Telling a lie about someone damages the person's character, destroys trust between the two, and makes it impossible to have a healthy relationship going forward, because a lie casts a dark stain on one's image or personality. In fact, lies negatively work both ways: they destroy the character of the ones who dishonestly tell lies, and later on, they destroy the character of the ones who believe what they hear without question. Then, they destroy the character of the innocent about whom lies were told. Like one stone that kills three birds at the same time.

Facilitating lies, let us call it rumors, is also problematic when facilitators make liars feel comfortable in their actions, as long as they take the lies to where they want them to go. Not to mention destroying others' relations, characters, and reputations. Their flattering attitude as excellent listeners sends a signal of what they can use in their future lying adventures. Liars know what to say and when to say it to manipulate others' emotions and actions, and by studying their audience, they know what they are more likely to believe. They know what the person they are lying to and the person they are lying about despises the most. They know where it is going to have an effect; they know when and where it will hurt the most. Liars never expose their true character; they know exactly what to say and the expected boomerang effect of their falsehood. Liars thrive on being associated with friendly and honest groups, while they display a charming attitude and charisma that prove to only be a cover-up for their misleading personalities. That is part of their character, to destroy others' character.

Imagine what a person who truly despises corruption would feel when he or she is falsely accused of being corrupt! Enough to cause them to choke, but even though most will not care to believe or not believe, the false accusation leaves a stain, nonetheless.

For those who do care, they may have failed to ask, "is it true?" Others distance themselves from the falsely accused person, the victim, the one they have known for a very long time as a righteous person, and then all of a sudden everything stops, and the relationship ends, and there's nothing left. Not only does the cycle go on, but it affects everything else in the process.

Lying often sounds like a cry for help; not only does it hurt the liar's character, but it also hurts the characters of the people around. When a person is hurt from the inside and wants to hide the negative consequences and portray a different image, to portray a good character that does not exist, hurting may breed anger that leads to a state of having to lie. The intention to lie may not always be a bad one, or the person telling a lie may not always be aware of telling a lie. But no matter the case, standing strong, and building confidence and courage to manage anger may help resist the force of telling a lie.

Two different signs inform our understanding of the lies we experience from other people. Sometimes, the lie comes from their *inner self*, which drives their inner conflict. At other times, the lie comes from the outside world, triggered from outside circumstances themselves. While the inner lie can affect their outside world and vice versa, interaction can be pivotal in the person's character, self-estimation, and inner conflict. In other words, one may lie about a specific person out of envy, intending to destroy what makes their character good. The influence of the inner envy pushes the lies out toward the person they have targeted to destroy.

Very often, intentionally or not, liars tend to create their own existence out of trying to make the targeted person insignificant or meaningless. This ignites a battle to overcome their character of lies while assassinating others' characters. Should we say lying is murder? Maybe, if lying can kill a person's image and character. Lying makes others believe what is not true. It creates a different perception of views, things, or others. If lying does not kill physically, it at least does so morally, emotionally and spiritually, because it can transform and change position and views, as well as destroy a part of who the person is.

With that said, when a person tells a bad and untrue story about another person, the result may be the destruction of something, a relationship, a business, an opportunity. Intentionally or not, sometimes, the lie offered is the best the giver can give or is considered a 'best guess' in a given situation. The problem may be the 'best guess,' because the rule should not be a guess but the truth, verified. And why guess when people can take the time to ensure what the truth is? Of course, our understanding of the world and humanity is constantly evolving and changing, but that does not exclude verification because, without verification, the consequence can be devastating in many ways including to one's character. Questioning what we know, read, hear, and research is a paramount consideration because a peaceful society and the well-being of the people depend on it.

When lying is a habit, it also becomes a character trait that lowers the category regarding integrity, principles, and value to others. One of the negative effects of a lie is the deterioration of trust, the destruction of one's image. Lies will probably never be completely erased and will always have a negative impact on lives, but the constant state of being lied to, and about, is one of the most torturous experiences a person can have. Lies are the main reason people with good character tend to distant themselves from those with bad character to move toward those they trust. Choosing to tell the truth and nothing but the truth instead makes someone stand out as a person of integrity with a sense of respect, leadership, and guidance. At least to tell the truth and nothing but the truth remains the rule. The result of which portrays a life of peace.

The Truth-Based Alternatives to Lies:

Some lies are built on lies, and lying to the self by denying what exists or what is true is a denial itself. It is sometimes known as 'burying our heads in the sand,' for example, not recognizing the wrongs, or accepting, confronting, and attempting to change bad habits or resolve behaviors that have become a problem. Also, for example, refusing to recognize as a lie something that has been propagated for a long time as truth, a denial that is common where addiction or dysfunction prevail. Lies get built on lies because dysfunction is not addressed. Then, the liars attempt to make others believe the fabricated new truth, creating an alternate reality in an attempt to divert the criticism or anger of others. Denial is a problem, but then it becomes gaslighting, in other words, making others believe a truth intended to justify the unhealthy or destructive consequences of the lies. And the solution is facing the truth with courage and asking what the problem is, how to resolve it, and honestly proceed to resolving the problem. Then, denial is resolved by building honesty about the denial and confronting the gaslighting stories that come with it. As long as common sense does not become a factor of criticism or judgment, whether it matters or not, the truth will be appreciated, and trust will increase as a result.

Breaking Promises with Lies

As a failure to keep a spoken or written commitment or promise, broken promises can be especially damaging when the person breaking the promise did not intend to keep their word in the first place, whether the promise was a lie, or the reason for the breaking was a lie. Nonetheless, it might be impossible to keep a promise, but if that impossibility becomes an alibi, it still is lie. Why make promises that cannot be kept? It must be to get away with something! It could be a double betrayal. Not only has the betrayer falsely raised others' expectations, but they have also changed their plans and thoughts; when the promise does not materialize, their plans change for a second time. The action of breaking a promise itself is inconsiderate and hurtful. Whichever way it is looked at, it is unethical and deceiving behavior. On the other hand, the promisee relying on the promisor truly believes that the promise will be kept, whether or not the promisee has taken every step to determine if the promise is valid.

Solving broken promises requires not making a promise unless there is an assurance to follow through. Circumstances and people do change; if that happens and the promise cannot be honored, timely communication can change the game and reset the pledge. Also, communication can spell out a form of apology for raising others' expectations, making amends, and defining new parameters rather than leaving them in a dire situation. In other words, devising a message that conveys an apology for having lied. These are cases where, whether we ask the question or not, we still end up in a situation where the promisor decides to change.

The omission of truth is the same as committing a lie. The truth is often omitted by communicating only a partial reality and by keeping the whole truth from others. Double deceptions are common in this digital era, as much as it is easy to 'cheat' emotionally. The behavior of omitting the truth is as consequential as a lie and can cause the same amount of damage. Lies of omission are common in business, especially in business formation and advertisement. There are instances of businesses that failed at a very early stage when many people pretended to be fully committed to a business partnership while putting their primary efforts elsewhere, or just collecting funds for ends other than for the intended business. They also tell half-truths to get into a position of power or advantage while acting in a spirit of equality. They play dishonest activities to deceive potential partners that may end in a financial hole. Because this has to do with money, it may have become the business model or money laundering scheme of the 21st century. The Bernie Madoff story is a great example of a man who did the above, deceiving the masses for a purported business that ended up ruining potential partners. Small business owners have silently copied the model and frequently seek to defraud potential investors. A solution may lie in asking if anything is true and seeking palpable evidence of authenticity.

When lies come as a misdirection, they are shared unintentionally but deliberately misleading; they become a deflection of the truth. As another form of misinformation, it is designed to divert attention from the real issue, often putting another person in a more defensive and weaker position. Some wrongdoers anticipate the victim's reaction by making it sound as unethical as theirs. The wrongdoers leave others unable to recognize who the real dishonest person is between the wrongdoer and the victim. This action may be devastating at the receiving end, to the extent that it can destroy the credibility and livelihood of the victim.

This example of misdirection is around the corner in our everyday lives. Sounds like the example of an in-law who makes sure you do not have access to your relative but goes ahead and makes the world think that you are the problem, surely the perpetrator blaming the victim. Also, we cannot forget when most politicians put the blame of their failure on their opponent to fool the constituents, while being reluctant to take responsibility, then at the same time promising to do better. And constituents often fall for the scheme, like believing in one side of the story. But it is not enough to be aware of one side of the story and seek the other side to complete the story, it is important to get educated on some subjects, like politics, and not solely rely on what is told because it is not always what you hear.

Making up lies, starting rumors, or telling others something dubious is another form of misdirection because it leads to larger rumors that may damage character and reputation, and also jeopardize positions and power. Due diligence is often bypassed but is key to finding solutions to misdirection and truth. In the case of business, a 'shiny penny' of financial gain can divert anyone from others' ethics or true character, but due diligence can lead in the right direction. Also, dirty politicking and the smearing of character, reputation, and power, as it is often played, is absolutely not worth the cause. But good counsel may ethically guide the perpetrator's position, while deterring his actions and by strengthening and protecting the victims from such schemes.

A bare-faced lie also is a cover-up that everyone knows is a lie. It is simple and cute at the same time for a little child to lie about not eating chocolate, even though there is a drippy mess all over his or her face. As the child gets older, he becomes more sophisticated with the cover-ups. Unfortunately, some people never grow up and deal with their lying habits. When their actions are uncovered, everyone, including the person telling the lie, resents the disrespect that it brings. Surely the scenario destroys trust and credibility, even if the lie was not malicious. Cover-ups are common in business in spite of the many individuals who can achieve success with their sociopathic disregard for the welfare of others. These individuals often thrive on bullying, intimidation, and the confusion they create no matter what it takes to make profits.

Some examples are often found in the Hollywood industry. Let us not have the misfortune to encounter some sociopaths as well as compulsive liars who are often motivated by a need for attention, while they find it difficult to refrain from doing what they do consistently, simply lying. A compulsive liar lies even when the truth would be easier and better to tell. He tells a lie in the face of the truth and for no reason. It appears to be a leisure where he finds pleasure but undermines what effect his behavior has on his character or personality A compulsive liar struggles with the truth, with authentic connection, and lacks compassion, but also undermines the effect their behavior on their personal character or personality.

They want what they want and go for it and, of course, with lies.

When it comes to lies of perception, it depends on the intention; they begin when we all tell ourselves stories or 'versions of the truth' we know, which is what 'lies of influence or perception' are about. The intention is what matters. In the business of selling services, for example, it is ethical and honorable to influence others' perceptions, so they understand the value of what is being sold and choose to buy it. The advertising and marketing industries thrive on this in the game of influence. They influence the consumers' views of the products and manipulate them into buying those products. On the other hand, manipulation plays a role in the perception of truth and deceitful or underhanded behavior, which includes 'old school' high-pressure sales tactics in which lies of influence and perception can quickly be destructive.

At a personal level, 'versions of the truth' often create conflict with one another. There may be different opinions of the same thing, understanding that life, unlike math, is not fixed and rigid. The key here is to accept and be tolerant of opposing views or opinions but rigid about the underlying ethics, values, and truth. Anything, including lies that create an unfair advantage to someone at the expense of another, is morally wrong and will eventually have an adverse effect, which can only be resolved with the truth. A meaningful dialogue toward win-win solutions and fair exchange of value, which should be sought, should always prevail over the distorting effect of lies.

When a lie is exaggerated, the people whose egos drive them, seek competitive advantage by magnifying anything they can use to come across as 'super,' trying to inspire envy or disbelief in others. Such behaviors portray more insecurity than they appear, an unattractive character flaw instead. Many may argue that lying is human nature as well; as the fallen from God's very commandment, humans lie for one reason or another, but it is up to others to ask themselves if it is true, so they don't become victims or facilitators of the mischief of exaggerations and lies.

Exaggeration is certainly not necessary to embellish the truth. Human authenticity is enough to convince us of ourselves. Telling the truth and watching others be drawn to it, like moths to a flame, should be a motto to combat humans' lying habit. Society will become magnificent as people continue to say only what is true, and also always making sure that what is being said is true.

9

THE PHYSICAL AND EMOTIONAL EFFECTS OF LIES

"Lying is like alcoholism, though you are always recovering."

– Steven Soderbergh

The *"Science of Honesty"* review by the American Psychological Association suggests that lying can cause serious risk of health, anxiety, depression. And surely this is the work of the specialists who own the details. The fact that lying can be physically and emotionally taxing explains its very nature. It must be a heavy exercise to lie, though lying can cause poor relationships and poor work performance. Sir Walter Scott wrote about "the tangled webs we weave" when people begin to lie or deceive others. The evidence of this with infamous people who get tangled up in their web of lies is palpable. Infamous people like sport figures or politicians may have their reputation affected in many ways. While sports figures often use performance-enhancing products as a way to level the playing field in a sport and lie about it, politicians make promises they cannot keep and tell the constituents what they want to hear, only to attract votes. It demonstrates how lies emotionally affect others to act the way they do, and very often, they are led in the wrong direction.

Lying affects the state of politics, and the future of the constituency politicians represent. As it turns out, lying can also affect the health and longevity of the people at the receiving end as a victim or a third party. Also, it can affect the mental health of the people consuming the lies. Lying is a combination of creating physical and emotional problems that feed each other. So, telling lies affects human health in general and particularly the health of an innocent person as a victim of the false and damaging information perpetrated toward his character or reputation. While many people who tell lies to get their way may not realize that the act itself is an emotional exercise that can become a poison capable of destroying one's health, many others do understand the consequences clearly but do so out of naughtiness or wickedness, as if destruction is the main goal behind their lies.

Lying creates stress both in the mind and the body, demanding physically and emotionally of all the people in the chain. A lie that leads to another, then another, can create a nerve-wracking cycle that becomes harder to keep track of and severely affects the health of the victim. Lying affects health conditions in many ways as it directly affects emotions, leading to anxiety and depression, which co-exist because the same or similar factors may be the cause. The bottom line is that difficult health conditions become persistent or inescapable with some concern that links the victims to a lie and how they feel bad about it. Most of those concerns and problems accelerate the feeling of depression when the exercise of lying becomes consistent. Not only can lying be the poison that endangers the health of the person doing the lying, but it also affects the health of the person who is the victim of the lie because it can take an emotional toll to process the lie at the receiving end.

Although lying is human, as it is said, everyone may have already experienced at one point that lying also hurts every aspect of our lives. It damages trust and keeps people apart from building meaningful relationships among themselves. The lack of trust increases the distance between individuals, making a relationship impossible or irreparable, and the emotions that come with the experience can be remarkable and damaging as well. Adding to the mix, being surrounded by lies is always as burdensome as it is unhealthy. Lying may seem like the easy way out of a situation that may cause a confrontation for many people, but the emotional effect rarely survives the challenge.

Some situations may decrease the chances of dealing with the challenges of emotionally surviving the lies and hurting themselves in the process but lies hurt in many ways. Imagine having to deny or justify the lies of others against you; while it may not be easy to keep control of your emotions, you may not be able to figure things out. While the emotions of dealing with the lies can be burdensome, the effects of the lies on the health of the victims cannot be measured. Therefore, understanding human nature, to begin with self-reflection, may be the right direction, prioritizing what is true.

The Mental Health Effects of Lies

Inasmuch as lying plays straight into emotions, and affects the mental state as a consequence, lying has gained a stronghold in modern culture. It appears to have become the new normal, lying and getting away with it; even the go-to for information, the news media, has become another source of lies. The constant narrative that is often repeated in the news plays a big role in feeding the listeners' minds, and whatever information is presented, accurate or false, may either satisfy or upset a number of people. Very often, the agitation seen on the streets by emotionally disturbed citizens, frustrated by some of the information given to them by the media, is in part the result. The result manifests with an epidemic of behaviors that can exacerbate mental issues because their minds become confused between what is true and what is not.

Often troubled and confused by the false information that continuously feeds the thread, citizens become agitated while making demands, and the confusion translates into intense agitation, though their motives remain questionable. When the mind is filled with false information, it can create mental issues; thus, information must be measured, studied, and reported accurately. The trend of protesting ignited by some way of reporting the news recently may have created confusion, anger, and ignited some agitation. Such confusion manifests in the disconnection from reality, the intersection between the different versions of the same story, the reaction to some versions deemed unacceptable, and the effects of disinformation. And this is because society has adopted a culture of lies and misinformation, unfortunately embraced by those who are supposed to inform the population. New technology has facilitated and multiplied the sources for information, as well as, unfortunately, misinformation that erodes public confidence. As people realize they are being lied to, manipulated, and misled, they resent it. And they do because it affects their mental health in some cases.

The devastating consequences of such confusion manifest as a mental illness, a trending crisis with the sources being ignored. When you think about the manifestation in the streets of major cities all over the world in recent years, very unpleasant situations occurred, and ignited an uprising. And it is often at the same time, hard to believe, as alleged, that law enforcement is assigned to chase down certain ethnic groups, not just criminals, but certain ethnic groups.

That alone is troublesome and can ignite frustrations. But the media did not help to tame down the narrative and the belief that it is the case, because the media is supposed to be the source of truth, but not anymore. Sometimes the impact of a situation depends on the narration that ignited it and that follows. When the narration is mixed with lies, it creates a different world. What happened in the summer of 2020 was atrocious, the allegation of 'racism' grew with no evidence, and the damages that ensued were unbearable.

When a person's mental state is affected and some situations arise unexpectedly, things become confrontational because of resentment. In the hopes that the confrontations do not end in a bad and irreparable act, lies and false information have conditioned a faction of citizens to be confrontational, with proliferation of fights and devastating consequences, yet all tied to a lie. The right solution in these circumstances becomes difficult with false information.

Fortunately, the press can do more as society expects, to promote positive messaging that can disentangle the vicious circle of reciprocated manipulation that has created a fallacy that destroys the minds of a faction of the population with the notion that they are being pursued. That alone driven by fabrications that anger instead of appease, contribute to mental health issues. But if only those factions can pause and reflect or take the time to have a meaningful dialogue, it can clear some confusion, diminish the impact on mental health in the process, and some situations may become less depressing and even less confrontational.

Mental health problem being on the rise is not surprising, as misinformation plays a role, because misinformation confuses. Other factors outside this scope may be contributory, but when those lies build up in the minds of those people, their first reaction when they encounter law enforcement is to confront, to fight, and the result may be fatal just as often. The crisis may be resolved beginning with civic education, compliance to, and respect of authority as an appropriate approach. And this too could help to avoid the crisis. What if people were more informed and not lied to? What if those people made an effort to ask themselves if the information they have is true? Society could be more peaceful.

When it comes to law enforcement encounters, compliance is better than confrontation, no matter the information or misinformation that is received. But if a person approaches a law enforcement officer with the right attitude, honesty, and truth, chances are there would be no altercation. Unfortunately, society is so ensnared in a web of lies and false information that exacerbates mental conditions and feeds confrontations. The lack of accurate information creates confusion that worsens the mental health of the people, especially when they are often reminded they are victims of a system that cannot help them. With the immeasurable consequences that come with misinformation and lies that manipulate the public, society could be better off if the truth and complete news were positively and accurately reported to avoid confusion and potentially ease the mental health of the people.

Mental health is an issue in a culture of lies that emerges with distorted reality, as if always being on constant alert and operating in emergency mode arouses public interest. Since the time of the recent pandemic when everyone thought the world was coming to an end, everyone ran to the news for a positive message of comfort. Unfortunately, with a scary situation that literally traumatized many, they did not find help, and mental health issues increased. The drama ensued with a manipulative perception of health and the processes for public policies, which included lying to the masses.

Unfortunately, the inaccuracy of the news creates even more confusion which does not help the mental health crisis but instead accentuates it. Seeking the truth and accurate information may help to maintain good mental health as effectively as eating healthily and exercising regularly, which is contrasted with having to seek conflicting information with news that only contributes to harming mental health by projecting more fear than positive messaging. Watching the news regularly increases the risk of anger, which activates the sympathetic nervous system, and therefore, attacks one's mental state because it is not favorable to maintaining good mental health.

There is a widening feeling that the news media have become unfair, contentious, and inaccurate. It may seem unthinkable that the news media could provide false or misinformation, which is more frightening, but humans run the news media, and humans lie. Again, the fear, the falsehood, and the inaccuracy of some news media truly confuse normal people. The strength and freedom experienced in telling the truth, or not being attached to a lie, or just having a peaceful mind, and the assurance the news fails to bring, even in the most difficult situations, can be an empowering feeling. Conversely, receiving accurate information or feeling vindicated also from false information could make people feel good mentally, emotionally, and spiritually and mend some aspects of a relationship in the process. Feeling good opens the possibilities of healing the mind and body, and not only does it diminish mental health issues, but it is also the truth.

10

THE IMPORTANCE OF DUE DILIGENCE

"All truths are easy to understand once they are discovered; the point is to discover them."

– Galileo Galilei

We live in a world of endless lies, where life is a race to the top and lies often play the escalator, where not only does information become propaganda and misinformation is designed to create confusion and distraction, but it is often labeled "fake news" whether the news is fake or not. But information is often taken at face value and at one's own peril. How to not make a single-story judgment is to question what is told, what people hear. Unfortunately, judgments are formed even before the information is completely delivered without asking if what is delivered is true or false, accurate or not, good or bad.

It is wrong to make such judgments that can redefine who others are, or misdescribe a dangerous product or any given circumstance. Almost every matter in modern society begins with a lie, whether it is in politics, business, science, relationships, or every other aspect of life. It is vulgarly called human nature, and lying has become the new norm. Despite the prescription of the values that characterize most societies, some of which were founded on the biblical principles, in which not everyone believes despite modern civilizations being founded upon them, but those principles define the truth. They define the truth as what conforms with fact or reality and the being of God. Not only does the principle define truth, but it condemns lies. And society has fallen for the latter.

It is hard to believe that "everyone lies," as they say, maybe not intentionally, but they do. Whether it is done by deliberate falsehoods, obfuscation, errors of omission, misdirection, denial, or by a long list of other reasons or justifications. I came across this quote that really makes sense: "Every lie we tell incurs a debt to the truth. Sooner or later, that debt is paid." The next time you are about to lie or participate in a lie, consider whether you are willing to pay the debt from the lie in the future. When a lie mischaracterizes a person, it means that the person has been misjudged based on a lie or a single story. This judgment causes damage that cannot be changed or corrected. Sometimes, such lies are insignificant ones that amuse only, but other times, they can be as significant as being able to destroy a livelihood.

When considering the latter group of lies, we can agree that it is vital to question what we know, what we hear, and be able to tell if we are being directed or misdirected, the right direction being the truth. This is a necessary step when having to make a decision, or any judgment, a judgment that can create some problems. Imagine a case of lies that can put all of society or a country in a wrong direction, like the case of lies that compromise health conditions. Imagine a case of lies that destroys relationships; it creates a chain of problems that affect individuals and society as a whole, from joblessness to single parenting, which comes with the ups and downs, the downs that often leave some children's upbringing difficult and with an uncertain future. A chain of problems that leave single parents discriminated against and even denied some opportunities, and so on. Sometimes, misinformation and lies can be entertaining because there is no intent to ask if it is true! It is simply entertaining to follow along as society does. Many examples of lies create circumstances and even crises that only truth can solve.

Other times, false information can be of deep significance and can negatively affect livelihoods because the false allegations were used to make a judgment. The failure to ask, is it true? and the lack of due diligence facilitates such ruination of livelihoods and creates other crises. One loss of employment or opportunity because a decision was made based on false information can ruin a family, and more, for the lack of due diligence, we understand what a lie can do. Many go their entire life with some unjust perception of bad reputation because someone someday decided to project a bad character with lies, because someone decided to describe other people with some bad name that they do not carry, simply out of dislike. Unfortunately, the whole entourage follows suit, maybe to please the crowd, but also for failing due diligence. Never have people ever asked if it is true, nor do they even know the person, or ever have an encounter with such a person. Yet they have heard they should despise the person, and they wholeheartedly do, believing they are doing the right thing, because modern society has taken people to that point, where they hate just because they should. It is called, in the Christian world, a fallen society. If you think about a famous political character, you will find an example.

The scientific ways of being lied to begin with the lack of doubt and questioning of what we hear. The tendency is to listen and agree, no matter the damage that it may cause. Until we know it is true, we have no judgment to make. This reminds me of one transition of power, during which the outgoing president knowingly took it upon himself to advise the incoming one to be careful with a particular choice as member of his cabinet because he thought he was "dangerous" but could have been a strength instead. After such a contentious election, should the incoming have taken that advice? The fake advice may have been a way of undermining the strength of the incoming administration, unless due diligence plays an important role. Those who tell lies know exactly where the lies will land, the effects they will have. They know where the train is going, while those who listen do not, yet they fail to find out until they suffer the consequences. The case may have been one of an administration of power, but it can also be one of a relationship or friendship in most cases where lost friends suffered one way or the other. Nevertheless, lies often create a loss: a loss of advantage and a loss of good reputation; and also, a single-story judgment should not lead to that point, but unfortunately it does. Ending a relationship is another example as compared to an error from an administration. The worst effects of single-story judgment affect lives, a crisis in society, and the cycle never ends. Also, it is difficult to forget the wars orchestrated by the lies, all the lives that have been lost, the amount of money that was spent, and the damage that the wars did, the cycle never ends. It is easy to make assumptions of the truth in most conditions, but assuming the truth in every situation is why we fail to question what we know and hear, and why we fail to question whether it is true.

Centuries ago, the earth was believed to be flat until science proved it was wrong, and it changed people's minds. Going from 'knowing' one thing to correcting it to something else, made minds change forever.

Understanding science teaches us to question what we know or hear, and also tells us more about what we think we know. The same is true for lying. Whether the science that came up with the earth was not flat after all was true, it made us change our minds without asking if it was true. Yet, we believe it because we are convinced with facts. If only liars could convince with facts, their lies would not succeed or have any impact; but they do not, because they expect others to just believe, and they always do.

Sometimes, what people have known to be true is not always true; questions begin to be asked whether what we know is true, and the need to make other judgments or decisions arises. Although experience is necessary but not systematic, knowing things based on selective observation or overgeneralization is not the truth, and experience also may involve many areas of life experiences, including upbringing, education, social ways, and more.

Parents undoubtedly teach children to avoid that hot stove. "If you touch it, you could get burned." That is the lesson, and that is what people have known to be true. Even with these warnings, children often touch the stove and experience the painful feeling of a burn, trying to defy what the parent told them, not because they want to know if it is true, but because they are stubborn in their own way. It is the result of a curiosity that drives children. As children, they are often influenced by their peers, who may lie to them. They are also influenced by social media feeds, with information that can be false, yet they do not always ask if it is true.

How we come to gain knowledge of the truth as a simple observation of our surroundings, which convinces us of what is. Sometimes, we have 'selective observation' and only see what we want to see, or make an assumption based on the only patterns or examples we have experienced in our lives; this also limits our ability to see the complete facts. Additionally, the information we receive from any source, supposedly accurate, often shapes our beliefs about what is true; but personal research can help discover more and what could be true or not true.

In summation, the many ways that people come to find out what they know is true can be reliable and not very reliable too. Being aware of the sources of knowledge helps to evaluate the accuracy and truthfulness of such knowledge we hear and hold, and the question of whether it is true is answered. Thinking about the truth, it is understood and believed to be what it is, the fact of what has actually occurred and not what someone said or thinks it is.

In information science, ontology deals with one's analytic philosophy of the nature of reality. Thus, sociology teaches us to believe that reality is in the eye of the beholder and that our job is to understand others' views of reality. While there may be different perceptions of reality, there is only one *true* reality. Meanwhile, epistemology teaches us *how* we come to know what is; and what should be called the truth. The way to uncover knowledge begins with asking ourselves if it is true. Without discounting the epistemological perspective, even public opinion may also contribute to how we come to find what is true.

When trust becomes a factor, the people we trust the most and go to with questions play a role as a source for due diligence. The problem is, if they are convinced that many others rely on them for answers, guidance, and information, then anything they say can be jeopardized in some circumstances with lies and manipulations. I can think of situations of broken engagements and divorce, bad business deals, wrong political moves, war. Had they done any due diligence, lies may have been found out, perhaps relationships may have been preserved, war may have been avoided, and more. Most lies come from these circumstances when the person who gives information is trusted. Thus, due diligence can even lead to another set of lies, so it's more suitable not to make any judgment based on what we hear but what we have witnessed firsthand to the truth.

There was a time when we made a bad decision based on the information we had at the time and we had buyer's remorse. It might have been making a wrong move, making a bad purchase. It could also have been the act of entering into a deceitful agreement, casting a vote based on false promises and lies. Or perhaps a decision was made, believing in something only to discover it was not true.

Sometimes, you may have to ask yourself:

- What caused that decision?
- What contributed to the error in making that assumption or decision?
- How did due diligence fail?
- How do I overcome the possibility of committing the same errors in the future?

Unfortunately, mistakes happen; most people make bad decisions occasionally. Professionals in their industry are taught how to ask questions as part of their development, but few think of questioning as a skill that can be improved upon, like considering how the questions are answered and how that could make the conversations more productive and get to the truth. For some, natural inquisitiveness, emotional intelligence, and the ability to read others put the ideal question forth. It is important to go deeper into due diligence while avoiding jeopardizing the trust that exists and is at play. The good news is that by asking questions, we naturally open our minds, improve our emotional intelligence, and become better versed in recognizing what is truth and what is not. It is also important to draw insight and learn from behavioral science to proceed with due diligence that influences the answers to the questions.

Listening becomes essential as a tool for judgment in the due diligence and verification process as well as being vigilant. Listening is essential as it helps to decipher

the conflicting forces that feed the belief that we know everything and what we do not.

In the process of seeking the truth, questions may remain as to what's needed to ask or explore to find the truth. In the previous example, I referred to a conversation with the King, during which I had to answer his investigative questions. What struck me the most during such a conversation was his attention to my answers. Listening carefully to what I had to say truly showed the eagerness to find the truth, the eagerness to comprehend, as my answers were very important for his judgment.

With the inconvenience of assuming, assumption can be in the first sense of finding what is the truth. But truthfulness is also wrongfully assumed. People are eager to impress others without the need to doubt any acquiescence because their conviction is based on the premise that everything they have assumed to be true is fact. Yet complacency prevents others from hearing anything else, but good questioning leads to uncovering more than what's already known, understanding the process and discovering the truth. While the questions are within the prospect of due diligence, the best approach to finding the truth through questioning depends on what information is being sought, with a goal to reach the level of accuracy of the information received; whether it will be useful to make any judgment or not, it will help to get to the truth. And as well, the process helps to uncover the other side of a story.

The bottom line is to get accurate information and facts necessary in making any judgment, and to avoid the confinement of a single-story judgment, because it has been proven to be misleading and damaging. Also, due diligence helps to seek the truth while preserving a secret at the same time, as it is important to consider that some information cannot be shared.

Some information can be damaging and must be carefully shared, but it would be less damaging to refuse to answer a question revealing negative information than to answer affirmatively. In other words, it would be less damaging as long as the other side of the story is uncovered, and the truth is established, though the information must be useful one way or the other. This takes us back to the law school years when I had to update the professor with my discussion with classmates in order to be reevaluated. Had he considered asking to hold a discussion with the group to clarify the nature of the preparation, he would have gotten the full scope of the story, and I may have been qualified for the missed opportunity at the time, had the evaluation not gone wrong because of the lies, and had the reevaluation taken place on time. The verification of information, the other side of the story, or simply seeking the truth, can be demanding in making sure information is protected, privacy is maintained, but it should be done mostly for important causes.

Albert Einstein once said, "Question everything," which means we must be willing to seek out new and true information and question what we know and hear. Thus, questioning everything is the process of getting to what is true. Questions and answers, reading, and researching, have power that goes far beyond due diligence. When society has been perverted with lies and values laxity to research the other side of the story, to research the truth, to the point where questions and answers have been relegated to irrelevance, truth appears to have become a thing of the past. The wellspring of all questions is wonder, curiosity, and a capacity for delight and, after all, due diligence. We pose and respond to queries believing that the magic of a conversation will produce a whole greater than the sum of its parts. The magic of a conversation will produce accurate information and truth. Sustained personal engagement and motivation require that we remain mindful of the transformative peace of asking and answering questions. This will help us restore a culture of lies, knowing that our words have power as we ask ourselves in any circumstance, "Is it true?"

"When you finally understand that it is important to stop following the lies and seek the truth, you will be disciplining yourself to do what you know is right and important, although difficult, is the high road to pride, self-esteem, and personal satisfaction."

– Prime Minister Margaret Thatcher,
United Kingdom

ABOUT THE AUTHOR

Born in Cameroon, Africa, Sylvie Nomeny is an author, a lawyer, a speaker, a consultant, and is passionate about girls' education in Africa. Girls in rural areas of Africa are partially excluded from education, and those in urban areas are limited in their ability to receive such education, not because of cultural resistance or unwillingness but on one hand, poverty plays a big role; on the other hand, corruption interferes and contributes to its limitation. The two hands play a great barrier to girls' education in Africa.

Living in the Washington, DC, metro area, Sylvie is a member of the American University—Washington College of Law alumni and a board member of the Organization International for the Political Advancement of Women in Africa (OIAPA), an organization with a mission to raise the participation, contribution, and influence of women in Parliament across Africa, in the hopes to be the voice of the unheard, because women are better positioned to understand many aspects and impacts of the crises that affect society.

Not only has she contributed to the International Organization of Francophonie (OIF) project for girls' education funds in Africa, but has also participated in many colloquiums in Africa, including the first colloquium on basic and civic education in Cameroon.

Through years of experience, she has realized that society and the world are made of lies from all corners. She believes that people are presumed innocent until proven guilty, but society has assumed the opposite, where one is guilty until proven innocent, and the return to that 'innocent' status can be difficult even if later proven.

Whether we realize it or not, we are all affected by lies. But a solution to a better and peaceful society starts with us; it begins with one simple question: Is it true? This book will take you to where and how you can be part of the solution.

CONNECT WITH SYLVIE NOMENY

To book Sylvie to speak at your company, upcoming conference, retreat, meeting, or as a guest on your podcast:

Email: sylvieserge.nt@hotmail.com

Connect with Sylvie on social media:

LinkedIn: https://www.linkedin.com/in/sylvie-nomeny-ll-m-6594826/

Facebook: https://www.facebook.com/sylvienomeny

Instagram: @sylvie.nom

If you are a fan of this book, please tell others...

- Write about *A Culture of Lies* on your blog and social media channels.
- Feature Sylvie on your podcast or radio/TV broadcast.
- Suggest this book to your friends, family, neighbors, coworkers, and company leadership team.
- Write an authentic, positive review on Amazon.com.
- Take a selfie of you holding the book, then post and tag Sylvie on your social media channels.
- Purchase additional copies for your family, friends, colleagues, and governmental connections.

www.ingramcontent.com/pod-product-compliance
Lightning Source LLC
Chambersburg PA
CBHW052029030426
42337CB00027B/4931